Pamela Chalkley
July 1992
Buckfast Abbey

GW00726789

Cooking Apples

This book of recipes found its inspiration in the Orchards of Ampleforth Abbey; many have contributed to its making.

Gracewing.

Fowler Wright Books
Southern Avenue
Leominster HR6 0QF

Graceving Books are distributed

In Canada by
Novalis
PO Box 990
Outremont H2V 457
Canada

In Australia by
Charles Paine Pty
8 Ferris Street
North Parramatta
NSW 2151 Australia

ISBN 0 85244 1940
First edition 1982
Second printing 1982
Second edition 1990

Printed by Astec Press Limited, Unit 39, Portmanmoor Road, East Moor, Cardiff CF1 5EB

Telephone: (0222) 464614   Fax: (0222) 493422

Contents

Preface

A very paltry gift, of no account
My father, for a scholar like to thee,
But Strabo sends it to thee with his heart.
So might you sit in the small garden close
In the green darkness of the apple trees
Just where the peach tree casts its broken shade.

De Cultura Hortorum

Walafrid Strabo, Abbot of Reichenau
9th century

In an essay on the mission of St Benedict John Henry Newman describes how, as Benedictine monasticism spread north and west across Europe, ". . . by degrees the woody swamp became a hermitage, a religious house, a farm, an abbey, a village, a seminary, a school of learning, and a city." And, he might have added, a garden. Monastic documents and plans, and the accounts of travellers and pilgrims, record more than a thousand years of horticultural activity in Benedictine communities. In the twelfth century, for example, the Benedictine chronicler William of Malmessbury wrote of the abbey of Thorney, in Cambridgeshire, that it was set in a Paradise (ie., a garden), surrounded by green grass and apple-bearing trees.

The contribution of the black monks to the preservation of classical learning after the final collapse of the Roman empire is well known, as is their role as the schoolmasters of early medieval Europe. Less familiar, perhaps, is their claim to be the leading horticulturalists and farmers of the western empire that was forming beyond the Alps in the eighth century. When Charlemagne sought to consolidate his new realm, centered on the Rhineland and Gaul, he turned to the Benedictines for their organisational and educational skills. These thus came to serve the purposes of the state in a way that St Benedict himself could never have envisaged. The development of systematic, innovative horticulture and agriculture was one aspect of this civilizing movement.

We know from Pliny that the Romans possessed great skills in the cultivation of plants for medical, dietary and aesthetic uses. They established gardens, orchards and farms throughout their empire, preferring to settle where the lie of the land and the climate made such activities practicable. In England they grew many crops, including wine-making grapes, and they probably introduced cultivated apples for cooking and eating, scorning the sour native species. However their advanced horticultural techniques fell out of use -along with other admirable technologies such as under-floor central heating - as the large villa estates crumbled into subsistence farms. From time to time, in the sixth and seventh centuries, a villa site was resettled by a small monastic community. Several of the early religious houses of southern England and Gaul were founded on such sites, and the monks no doubt enjoyed the fruits of the apple orchards that are still such a distinctive feature of south-western England and northern France.

However it is not until the ninth century that it is possible to form any clear picture of the place of horticulture in Benedictine monastic life as it evolved under Charlemagne and his successors. Suddenly we are in a bright sunlit world of gardens and gardeners: the ideal monastery depicted on the Plan of St Gall has two gardens, for medicinal plants and vegetables, and an orchard that is also the cemetery; Walafrid Strabo, abbot of Reichenau, is writing a long poem about gardening; and St Benedict of Aniane, a leading figure at the imperial court, is swapping cuttings with the English monk Alcuin, who by then was abbot of Marmoutier, just outside Tours. It seems likely that it was Benedict who compiled the list of plants in the **Capitulare de villis**, the document that prescribed in detail how the imperial estates and towns were to be constructed and administered. The **Capitulare** lists 89 species of plants, not all of which would have grown in northern Europe. It includes named varieties of apples - Gozmaringa, Geroldinga, Crevedella and Spirania - as well as such familiar categories as Sweetings, Sour Apples, Keepers, Earlies, and apples to be eaten as soon as ripe.

Walafrid Strabo's poem **De Cultura Hortorum** reveals a fund of knowledge about the methods and problems of cultivating a variety of plants, based on careful observations of their needs and habits, and of their diseases. This precise and practical approach, combined with a keen appreciation of the wonderful complexity and ultimately the mystery of the natural world, is characteristically Benedictine. The Reichenau peninsula, jutting out from the north shore of Lake Constance, is ideally suited to horticulture, with fertile easily worked soil, adequate moisture, and plenty of sunshine. It is no surprise to find that today it is covered with market gardens.

The monks are no longer there, but the abbey church, which in part dates back to Walafrid's time, stands among fields of leeks, onions, peas, beans, cabbages and other vegetables, and the many greenhouses shelter tomatoes, peppers, melons and squashes - cousins of the gourds about which he wrote an entertaining and sharply observed passage.

Monastic gardens and plantations thus have a long history, and the traveller with an understanding eye will find plenty of evidence of the continuity of Benedictine horticultural activities over more than a millenium. These activities have always been rooted in practical necessities, amongst which may certainly be included gardens for refreshment and contemplation, and gardens to provide flowers and plants to deck the altars, as well as gardens for medicinal and culinary plants. The monastery garden beloved of Pre-Raphaelite painters and Victorian ballad-writers is however largely a figment of nineteenth-century sentimentality. There is no evidence that cloister gardens, in particular, harboured anything much in the way of plants beyond an area of grass and a few clipped trees and low evergreen hedges. The documentary and archaeological evidence suggests that while most monasteries had a small garden or herber for medicinal plants within the enclosure, and possibly also a sitting and strolling area near the infirmary, the main vegetable gardens and orchards were outside the inner precinct. The Gaye at Shrewsbury, the setting of many key episodes in Brother Cadfael's detective work, was one such extra-mural area, and there are still apple trees growing on the site.

The plant lover who wants to see what monastic gardens were - and are - like must go in search of them. It is an enjoyable chase, best pursued in Normandy, where monks and apples still flourish, and where the cooking is largely based on apples and cream. There are some Norman recipes in this book. The gardens of present-day Benedictine communities such as St Wandrille, on the right bank of the Seine near Caudebec, and Le Bec-Hellouin, on the river Risle further south, are not all visible to the public, for obvious reasons. Others are however being restored, for example at St Martin de Boscherville a little way downstream from Rouen, where the abbey gardens surrounding what is now the parish church are being restored to their seventeenth century splendour. A plan dated 1683 shows the enclosed hillside laid out with formal beds in which are planted carefully spaced trees, probably apples, and it is to be hoped that when the terracing and restoration of the pools and fountains is complete, replanting will follow.

Only last summer I came across a small priory near Livarot, now being restored and replanted by its loving owners. Besides modest gardens and a small orchard the priory boasts a large cider press, housed in an imposing black-and-white timber building with a steeply pitched russet tiled roof. It consists of a large circular stone trough, about five metres in diameter, round which a horse-powered wheel once slowly revolved, *squeezing out the apple juice which flowed down into a central drainage channel and away into the butts in which it was fermented and matured. Now the press is filled with potted plants, but standing in the doorway of the building, looking out over the little Norman pastures dotted with old apple trees, it is easy to imagine how busy it must have been at harvest time in its heyday.*

It is thought that Norman monks brought the art of cider making to England. Many of the old Benedictine houses of the south and west were originally founded from the great abbeys of Normandy, and in Somerset, Gloucestershire, Herefordshire and the Welsh borders monastic sites and apple trees abound. Cleeve, Llanthony, Deerhurst, Kilpeck, Abbey Dore – the names invite exploration. For a sight of a contemporary Benedictine orchard on a large scale it is necessary to travel to Ampleforth Abbey in North Yorkshire, where what must surely be one of the most northerly apple-growing enterprises in Europe is to be found. A brief account of its creation and cultivation follows, written by Dom Edmund Hatton, monk of Ampleforth, lover of apples, and the originator of this cookery book.

Feast of St Jane Frances de Chantal   Caroline Miles
12 December 1990   Chadlington
Oxfordshire

Introduction

Monastic tradition has it that the Ampleforth orchard was first planted by Abbot Smith somewhere about 1900. It included among its varieties Annie Elizabeth, Bismarck, Cockpit (both Yorkshire and Improved), Lord Grosvenor, Newton Wonder and Transparente de Croncels. Of these trees only one, a Lord Derby, still survives just outside the Procurator's office. Some grubbing and replanting took place during and just after the war, but it was the arrival of Bert Skinner in 1955 which was the turning point. He came with years of experience of apple growing in Essex and he worked with great dedication for 18 years. Because of his presence the size of the orchard was more than doubled with the planting up of Cherry Tree Field with culinary and dessert apples, plums and soft fruit. Throughout his 18 years in the orchard Bert was helped and supported by members of the monastic community who took their share of the picking, pruning, spraying, hedge clipping, grubbing and planting. Bert's place has now been taken by Peter Richardson, still supported by members of the community.

Our aim has been to provide a succession of culinary and dessert apples to supply as much of the school and staff as possible for as long as apples would keep. We have never had a gas store. Hence the orchard contained a large number of varieties and especially those with naturally good keeping qualities. Time came when the trees were big enough to meet the needs of the school and our local green-grocer willingly took our surplus to sell. Output continued to increase and farm gate sales started.

This led to two developments. Firstly the start of a new plan of grubbing the 20 year old trees on MM104 and their replacement with newer varieties on a more intensive plant on M9. Secondly it led to the production of "Cooking Apples".

I must take sole responsibility for this idea. If we were willing to sell good cookers, then it would be a good thing to share the many excellent ways of cooking them. I contributed nothing myself. I begged and cajoled recipes out of my friends, among them communites of Carmelite and Benedictine nuns. I then found I was too busy and anyway far too lacking in expertise to do either the time consuming preparation or the editing of what had by then grown into something much more comprehensive and expert than I had originally anticipated. The fact that "Cooking Apples" has ever seen the light of day is due entirely to the enthusiasm and time given at various crucial stages by Ida Mary Starr, Anne Burdett-Smith and Caroline Miles. But a most special word of gratitude to Caroline Miles. She became involved at moment of inertia and brought her invaluable energy, skill and experience to bear. She edited the entire book and saw it through from typed notes to the book you now hold in your hands. The title page was designed by a member of the community, Fr. Lawrence Kilcourse, and I am grateful to him for all the trouble he took at very short notice. My thanks, too, to Joan Morgan for her entertaining and informative essay on the various properties and uses of cooking apples. I want to thank as well everyone who so kindly contributed to this collection of recipes. I would like to mention each by name but my fear of omitting even one name and thereby causing sadness makes me hesitate to do this. I hope that all who did contribute will glow with satisfaction when this book arrives in their hands. They will know that even if they are not thanked by name, all the credit is theirs.

Finally I would like to make a request to all readers and users of this book. No doubt you will spot omissions and gaps in this collection of recipes, and you will have your own favourite recipes. There are blank pages at the back: jot down your own suggestions and send them to me for possible inclusion in the 3rd edition. Thank you so much!

Feast of St. Benedict,
11th July 1982.

Edmund Hatton, OSB
Ampleforth Abbey,
York, YO6 4EN.

Culinary Apple Varieties and their Uses

Joan Morgan

Most of the apples that were at one time highly thought of and grown throughout England can be found in the Royal Horticultural Society's Fruit Collection at Wisley in Surrey. The collection contains over 300 dessert apples and more than 200 culinary varieties. For the past several years Joan Morgan, the author of this essay, has been tasting and testing these apples with the help of the RHS Fruit Officer Harry Baker. To find out the flavour and cooking properties of this large number of different apples she devised a 'standard baking test'. Peeled slices were baked in sealed foil dishes for 15 mins at 200°C. Sadly only a small number of the 200 varieties are now available from nurserymen or grown commercially. Here she concentrates on those that are available from farm shops and green-grocers, though she also mentions some of the more interesting ones in the Wisley Collection. A more extensive account of her investigations has been published in the RHS journal THE GARDEN; on the culinary varieties in November 1980 and on the dessert varieties in August 1982.

Everyone is familiar with a Bramley but few now know of the immense number of different cookers that were once grown all over England, when Victorian connoisseurs gave as much serious consideration to apples as they did to their claret and port. Over dinner they not only argued the merits of Ribstons and Blenheims but had strong opinions on what was the best sauce apple or whether apple jelly made from Nonsuch was as good as that produced by Golden Pippin. Varieties like Herefordshire Costard, Carlisle Codlin and Yorkshire Goose Sauce were well known locally. In country districts for centuries Catshead, large and conveniently box-shaped, had been used to make the ploughman's apple dumpling. Norfolk Beefing dried well; eaten with sugar and cream Norfolk Biffins were a popular after dinner sweetmeat on sale in Norwich until the 1950s.

Using these old apples again it was clear that flavours and cooking properties could range from sweet to sharp and frothy to firm. While a Bramley is well suited to most of the recipes in this book it is interesting to consider the different requirements and see which other apples might be appropriate. Some recipes call for a stiff puree, others a light fluffy apple to fold in with egg white. A baked apple needs to cook well but not explode; for a French open tart the slices of apple must be soft and properly cooked but not disintegrate and ruin the design. A strong sharp fruity taste is needed to balance the richness of pastry which can overwhelm a light and delicately flavoured apple.

All apples have a fair amount of acidity. Even dessert apples would be cloying and characterless without it. Culinary apples have more, and the amount of acid determines their cooking properties. The more acid the more readily they cook, too little acid and the apple will cook poorly. The structure of the flesh is another factor. Thus the summer apples like Early Victoria that size up quickly and contain lots of water cook easily to a froth, but slices of the tough fleshed late varieties tend to keep their shape. With keeping acidity falls, sugar content rises and flavour mellows, fading towards the end of a variety's season. All these changes affect the way an apple cooks. For example a Bramley used very early in August or September will cook to a froth but taste very sharp with little flavour, in season, around Christmas, it makes a sharp fruity puree, and by the end of its natural storage life, in March or later still, it may even keep its shape and be sweet enough to eat raw or use in a vegetable salad. Apples stored in a controlled atmosphere, as many of those commercially available now are, do not age in this way and tend to taste and behave as they might have done when harvested.

The locality and the year will also affect the flavour of an apple and its cooking properties. For instance Cambusnethan Pippin, an old Scottish cooker, has little acidity grown in the Wisley orchard in Surrey, while the dessert apple James Grieve if deprived of sun will be too acid to eat raw but will cook well.

The season begins in August with apples like Early Victoria which cook to a light fruity froth, a little sharp but mild in comparison with a November Bramley. Baked Early Victoria is almost soufflé-like bursting into a juicy fluff and good for light airy dishes like Apple Snow. Grenadier used in August cooks to a puree but left on the tree until late September has a richer flavour and tends to keep its shape.

Lord Dudley, Foreign Secretary during the reign of George IV, is said to have never dined comfortably without apple pie, complaining audibly through grand dinners if his favourite delicacy was missing. He probably held equally strong views on the best apple to use. Edward Bunyard, nurseryman and connoisseur of the nineteen twenties and thirties, was in no doubt that Golden Noble fulfilled all his conditions. A late September/October apple, Golden Noble is perfectly cooked by the time the pastry is ready, soft and pale cream but keeping some of its form and not collapsing into a thin puree leaving a great void between the filling and the lid. It may need a little sugar but lemon peel and cloves are redundant, the flavour is sharp and fruity.

Lord Derby is also good for pies, sharp and fruity if used early in October, sweeter but faded by November and in my experience best used green.

Although rarely grown now, even in amateurs' gardens, Thomas Rivers is sufficiently interesting to be worth mentioning. It cooks to a juicy puree, sharp with an intense aromatic flavour; Bunyard described it as 'a distinct pear flavour with an almost quince-like acidity'. It makes a delicious apple sauce to complement pork or goose and it is also good for recipes such as baked red cabbage.

Bramley's Seedling comes into season by the end of October, and cooks to a creamy puree. It is sharp with a strong fruity flavour combining well with pastry. There are not many apples as sharp or robustly flavoured as a Bramley, though Dummelow's Seedling, better known as Wellington, was often recommended for making mincemeat; it cooks to a sharp fruity puree with good length and depth of flavour, and keeps well until February or March. Reflecting perhaps a time when sugar and exotic embellishments were scarce and expensive, many cookers are sweet and delicately flavoured, best suited to simple recipes: the September apple Mank's Codlin for example, and Byford Wonder, a handsome large golden apple with a fragrant delicate taste. Reverend W. Wilkes, another good looker, is quite sweet and well flavoured, while Beauty of Kent, the apple thought to have brought the idea of gravity onto Newton's head, is mild and gentle. Howgate Wonder and Newton Wonder are also lightly flavoured and sweet in comparison with a Bramley. The late keeper Annie Elizabeth too has much less acidity cooking to a lightly flavoured puree.

Apples that will keep their shape during cooking and have a rich flavour are hard to find as anyone knows who has tried to make an open French tart. Dessert apples if they have sufficient acidity will cook well, an early Cox, Orleans Reinette or Blenheim Orange for example. For the best dessert flavour a Blenheim must not be too big. According to the old enthusiasts in North Oxfordshire, where there are still some venerable trees, any fruit judged too large for dessert were sent back to the kitchen with the instruction that they be made into Apple Charlotte — a sensible recommendation as a Blenheim makes a stiff puree, quite sharp and fruity.

For making Tarte aux Pommes I am told pâtissiers in Paris use Reinette du Canada, which despite its name is an old Normandy apple usually thought of here as a dessert variety similar to a Blenheim but not so nutty, sweeter and more aromatic. Among the varieties that I tried Winter Queening, an old Sussex apple, was very good. It will make a stiff puree for lining the pastry base; the slices on top cook perfectly to an attractive yellow colour but do not fall apart and spoil the pattern. The flavour is sweet yet sharp and rich enough not to need anthing else. Purists can even make a glaze from the concentrated strained pulp of the peelings and core together with some whole fruit.

Earlier in October and November Transparente de Croncels was ideal for Tarte aux Pommes and for the more delicate combination of apples baked in a puff pastry shell. Originally from the North of France and still grown there, its cooked slices are a pretty yellow colour and richly flavoured. A late September Grenadier is also worth trying.

For savoury dishes using raw fruit well flavoured dessert apples are probably best though many cookers are sweet enough to use especially towards the end of their seasons. Most earlies are crisp and refreshing. Beauty of Bath, Miller's Seedling and Discovery, for example and later the classic dessert apples Cox's Orange Pippin, Orleans Reinette and Ribston are all possibilities. Many dessert apples have an intense flavour, sweet yet sharp, with an aromatic quality that reminds me of acid or fruit drops, and these are not overwhelmed by vinaigrette dressings or lost in a mixture of vegetables. In October and November Sunset and Holstein for example, and the old Gloucester apple Ashmead's Kernel in December and January, also in the New Year Tydeman's Late Orange and Suntan and a properly ripe Crispin is also worth trying.

Essentially one has to experiment and use what is available but it is worth bearing in mind that far from all being just cookers culinary apples can have as much individuality and interest as the better known dessert varieties.

Editorial Note

Some of the recipes in this book suggest the use of particular varieties of apples. With the help of Joan Morgan's article you may want to experiment with others. Cooking apples are as individual and interesting in their own way as the dessert varieties and, like English cheeses, many of them are due for a revival.

Several of the recipes call for butter. This may sound extravagant, but for the buttered apples on page 50, or the French apple tarts on page 23, margarine is not an adequate substitute. A knob of butter brings out the flavour of the fruit in a very special way. If you can't manage butter, turn instead to one of the many recipes where it is not essential.

C.M.

TEMPERATURE CONVERSION CHART

Regulo Mark	Farenheit	Centigrade
1	275	140
2	300	150
3	325	170
4	350	180
5	375	190
6	400	200
7	425	220
8	450	230

Savoury Dishes

"Cooking is one of those arts which most requires to be done by persons of religious nature."

A.N. Whitehead.

1   Normandy pheasant

1   Escalopes of veal with cream, calvados and apple

2   Huntingdon Fidget Pie

2   Himmel und Erde (German black pudding with apples)

3   Grilled pork chops with cider sauce

3   Fried apple and cheese sandwiches

4   Gammon with marmalade and apple glaze

4   Savoury stuffed apples

5   Sweet-sour red cabbage

5   Parsnips and apples

6   Twelfth Night Pie

7   Smithfield ham cooked with apples

Normandy Pheasant

1 large pheasant
6 large dessert apples - Cox or Reinette
3 oz butter
4 oz double cream
salt, pepper, cinnamon

Brown the pheasant in half the butter. Peel, core and slice the apples; fry them lightly in the rest of the butter, sprinkling them with cinnamon as they cook. Put a thin layer of cooked apples into a deep casserole, arrange the pheasant on top, breast down, and tuck the rest of the apples round the bird so that it is embedded in them. Pour in half the cream. Cover and cook in an oven, gas Mark 4/180°C, for about an hour, turning the bird breast side up at half time and seasoning it with salt and pepper. Remove the pheasant from the casserole, add the rest of the cream to the apple mixture and allow to heat through. Carve the bird and serve surrounded by the savoury apple gravy.

Keep the accompaniments simple - game chips and a watercress salad.

Escalopes of Veal with Cream, Calvados and Apple

4 escalopes of veal (1 per person)
1 large or 2 small dessert apples
4 oz double cream
butter, seasonings, Calvados

Peel the apples and cut into small cubes. Melt some butter in a heavy frying pan and brown the escalopes quickly on both sides. Add the apple cubes and cook for 2 or 3 minutes. Warm a small liqueur glass of Calvados in a little pan, set light to it and pour over the meat and apple cubes, shaking the pan until the flames die down. Transfer the meat to a warm dish, add the cream to the apple and juices in the pan and stir to heat through, scraping up all the delicious brown bits from the bottom of the pan. Season with salt and pepper. Arrange the cubes of apple on top of the escalopes, pour the sauce round, and serve at once.

Huntingdon Fidget Pie

1 lb cooking apples
½ lb onions
¾ lb streaky home-cured bacon
seasoning
8 oz shortcrust or flaky pastry

Peel, core and slice the apples. Cut the onions into rings. Dice the bacon.

Put a layer of apple in the bottom of a large pie dish, then a layer of onion and finally a layer of bacon. Sprinkle with salt and pepper.

Repeat until the dish is full.

Pour on about ½ pint of water and cover with a pastry crust.

Bake at Mark 3/170°C for two hours. Brush the pastry with milk and return to a hot oven Mark 7/220°C, for 10 minutes to brown the top.

Himmel und Erde
(German Black Pudding with Apples)

2 lb large potatoes
2 lb cooking apples
2 large onions
1 oz butter
pepper
2 teaspoons salt
4 oz caster sugar
4 oz lean bacon
1 lb black pudding

Peel the potatoes and cut into large slices. Cook with salt until tender.
Peel, core and quarter the apples. Simmer gently with sugar and a little water until soft.
When the potatoes are ready drain off and discard one third of the water. Mash the potatoes in the remaining water and beat smooth.
Add the apples and their cooking liquid and stir well.
Place over a low heat and simmer gently.
Peel and finely slice the onions and dice the bacon. Saute. Add to the potato mixture and season well.
Cut the black pudding into 2 or 3 pieces and halve lengthwise. Fry in butter. Serve apple and potato in a heated tureen with the black pudding.

Grilled Pork Chops with Cider Sauce

4 pork chops
3-4 shallots
salt, pepper, parsley
glass of cider

Chop shallots and parsley very finely and season with salt and pepper. Spread half the mixture over the chops, moisten them with a little oil or melted butter, and grill for 10 minutes or longer, depending on the thickness of the chops. Turn the chops, spread the rest of the shallot mixture over their other sides, moisten again and grill until cooked. Transfer the chops to a serving dish, and pour a glass of cider over the juices and bits in the pan. Reduce the sauce until it is quite thick, either by putting the grill pan over a flame or, if that is not practicable, transfering the juices and cider to a small saucepan. Pour over the chops and serve.

This makes a pleasant change from grilled pork chops with apple sauce. If you want more apple flavour, sprinkle a finely chopped sweet apple over the chops after you have turned them, and distribute the rest of the shallot mixture over the apple.

Fried Apple Sandwich

2 large Bramley apples or 3 large Crispin apples
2 oz butter
8 thin slices of processed cheese
8 slices sandwich loaf
fat or oil for frying

Peel and core the apples. Cut each into 4 thick slices and fry lightly in butter, turning once. Keep warm in oven. Remove crusts from bread. Spread with butter on one side and cover with a slice of cheese. Sandwich in pairs with a slice of apple in the centre. Press firmly together and fry in shallow fat until golden and crisp (both sides). Top each sandwich with a fried apple slice and serve immediately. Serves four.

Marmalade and Apple Glaze for Gammon

Gammon joint
4 oz marmalade (thick)
2 dessert apples
lemon juice

Simmer joint for half the cooking time. Strip off skin and bake at gas Mark 4/180°C until 20 minutes before end of cooking time. Meanwhile peel, core and slice apples and dip the slices in lemon juice. Warm the marmalade. Brush gammon joint liberally with marmalade and arrange the apple slices over the fat. Secure them with wooden cocktail sticks and brush remainder of marmalade over them. Increase oven heat to gas Mark 7/220°C and bake for 20 minutes, basting frequently.

Savoury Stuffed Apples

2 oz butter
4 shallots
½ lb pork fillet
clove of garlic (crushed)
1 tsp made mustard
6 large cooking apples
tsp Soy sauce
2 oz seedless raisins
juice of a lemon
4 oz demarara sugar
glass of white wine
salt and pepper

Melt the butter in a heavy saucepan, chop the shallots finely and cook for a few minutes. Cut the pork into ½ inch cubes and add to the shallots. Cook gently for 5 minutes. Add the garlic, mustard, soy sauce, raisins, lemon juice and sugar. Season well and add some of the wine. Cook the mixture gently for ½ hour, adding more wine from time to time.

When cooked core the apples, scoop out sufficient pulp from the centre to make a good cavity. Stuff apples with the mixture, stand them in a baking tin containing a little water, cover with greased paper and bake at Mark 4/180°C for about 20 minutes. The cooking time depends upon the apples. They should be just cooked through but not breaking up. Serve at once.

Sweet-Sour Red Cabbage

1 small red cabbage (about 2 lbs)
2 medium onions
2 cooking apples
2 tablespoons brown sugar
2 tablespoons port or sweet dessert wine (madeira,
sherry, marsala)
2 tablespoons wine or cider vinegar
bouquet garni
salt, pepper

Slice the cabbage thinly. Slice the onions and peel, core and slice the apples. Arrange the cabbage and the onions, mixed with the apples, in alternate layers in a deep oven proof casserole, seasoning as you go with sugar, salt and pepper. Put the bouquet garni in the middle. When the pot is full pour over the liquids and cover - if the lid is not tight-fitting, it is a good idea to cover with foil first - and cook for about 3 hours in a slow oven, gas Mark 2/150°C.

It improves with reheating. Excellent with pork, goose, hare, and sausages.

Baked Parsnips and Apples

1 lb parsnips, boiled and mashed
1 large cooking apple
1 tablespoon brown sugar
1 teaspoon lemon juice
1/2 teaspoon nutmeg
breadcrumbs

Peel, core and slice the apple.

Arrange the layers of parsnips and apple in a small casserole dish, finishing with a layer of apple.

Sprinkle with brown sugar, lemon juice, nutmeg and breadcrumbs.

Bake at Mark 4/180°C until the breadcrumbs are golden brown.

Serve with grilled bacon.

Twelfth Night Pie

Hot water crust:
6 oz lard
7 oz water (¹/₃ pint)
1 lb plain flour
salt

Filling:
2 lb chopped left over meats · turkey, goose, ham,
sausages. *Be sure to include some fat ham or bacon,
particularly if you have a lot of turkey to use up.
Chopped herbs, salt and pepper.*
¹/₂ pint (approx) jellied gravy or stock · add gelatine
if necessary
¹/₂ lb cored, chopped, unpeeled apple

A raised pie, for which you need a hinged pie mould
or a deep cake tin with a removable base.

To make the pastry, bring water and lard to the boil
and tip the boiling mixture into the seasoned flour.
Mix as rapidly as possible, and set aside until it is just
cool enough to handle. It must not be allowed to get
cold. Cut off about ¼ for the lid, and tip the rest into
the greased, floured mould. Quickly and lightly
shape the pastry up the sides of the mould, making
sure there are no gaps or cracks.

Put in the meat, seasoned with herbs, pepper, and
salt if needed. Cover with a layer of chopped
apples, and pour in the warmed stock or gravy.
Finally brush round the edges of the pastry case with
beaten egg and stick the lid on firmly. Cut a hole for
the steam to escape, and use the pastry trimmings to
decorate the top. Brush with beaten egg. Bake at
Mark 6/200°C for 30 minutes, and at Mark
3/170°C for a further hour. If you have used any
uncooked meat or bacon it may need rather longer.

For an alternative filling, if the Christmas leftovers
are all gone, use 2lb boned pork (shoulder or spare
rib), 2 oz unsmoked bacon, 1 large onion, salt,
pepper, nutmeg. Chop meat and onion coarsely
and season. Beat in ¼ pint dry cider or light ale. Fill
the pie case with alternate layers of this mixture and
chopped apple mixed with a tablespoon of brown
sugar and a little softened butter.
Bake as above, but give the pie at least 1¹/₂ hours at
the lower temperature to ensure the meat is properly
cooked.

Smithfield Ham cooked with Apples

To serve a party:
1 cured ham (approx 14 lb)
1½ lb cooking apples
1 lb soft brown sugar
¾ pint cider vinegar
4 oz soft brown sugar
4 tablespoons French mustard
1½ tablespoons dry sherry
whole cloves

Soak ham for up to 24 hours, changing the water at least 3 times to remove the salt. Wash in cold water and scrub with a stiff brush. Put ham in a large pan of cold water and bring to simmering.

Peel and quarter the apples and add to the pan with the brown sugar and vinegar. Partially cover the pan and simmer for 18 minutes per pound or until the small bone at the shank end can be removed. The ham should be covered by the water during cooking.

When ham is cooked and cool enough to handle, remove the skin and excess fat and score the remaining fat deeply into diamonds.

Mix brown sugar, mustard and sherry into a paste. Spread over the fatty surface of the ham. Stud each diamond with a clove.

Bake for 40 minutes at Mark 4/180°C, basting occasionally with the juices.

Cool and serve very thinly sliced.

Soups, Sauces, Stuffings, an Apple Garnish

"But by the red cheek never be misled;
For virtue, flavour, seek the acid green.
Of looks less kindly, but of sharp reward
Like stringent wit that keeps a matter keen."

V. Sackville West.

Apple Soup

Apple sauce (see page 9)
1½ oz butter
1½ oz flour
½ pt milk
½ pt water or light stock
salt and pepper

Make a white sauce in the usual way. If you have a light chicken or veal stock available it may be used instead of the water, but do not use a stock cube: the flavour is too strong.

Liquidize together with the apple sauce, dilute to soup consistency if necessary and check seasoning.

Serve hot.

Apple and Chestnut Soup

1 lb chestnuts in their shells
1 stick celery
2 large dessert apples (Cox or Reinette) peeled, cored and sliced
2 oz butter
3 pts light stock or water
4 oz single cream
salt and pepper

Prepare the chestnuts in the usual way. If you can't get chestnuts in their shells, or you haven't got time to prepare them, ½ lb dried chestnuts or a tin of chestnuts in water *(Marrons entiers au naturel)* make perfectly good substitutes.

Cook the chestnuts in half the stock, with the chopped celery, for about 20 minutes, or until the nuts are quite soft.

Meanwhile simmer the apple slices in the butter with a little salt and pepper. When both chestnuts and apples are soft, liquidize together and dilute to soup consistency. Check the seasoning, and just before serving add the cream and stir. Serve with fried croutons.

Cucumber and Apple Soup

2 large cucumbers
1 lb cooking apples
1 lemon
1 small clove garlic, crushed
1 glass dry white wine
salt and pepper
sour cream or natural yoghurt

Peel, core and slice the apples. Cook them gently in a very little water with the juice and grated rind of the lemon. Push them through a sieve or the medium disc of a Mouli-legumes; the puree should not be too smooth.

Put the apple puree into a large bowl and grate in the peeled cucumbers, using all the liquid but removing any large seeds. Sprinkle the mixture with sea salt and leave for at least two hours.

Add crushed garlic and wine, stir well and check the seasoning. A little fresh chopped dill or fennel makes a nice addition. Dilute if necessary.

Chill well and serve topped with a swirl of sour cream or a spoonful of yoghurt in each bowl.

Apple Sauce

1½ lb cooking apples
water
1 dessertspoon brown sugar
salt and pepper

Peel, core and coarsely chop the apples. Put into a heavy pan with a tablespoon of water and cook until soft, stirring occasionally to prevent burning. Flavour with brown sugar, salt and pepper.

These quantities should make a good pint of sauce - people always seem to eat the lot!

The flavouring may be varied by adding a couple of cloves to the apples while they are cooking (be sure to remove them before serving), or by substituting 2 tablespoons redcurrant jelly for the brown sugar.

Apple Sauce with Orange

1½ lb cooking apples
grated rind and juice of one small orange
1 oz butter
1-2 tablespoons brown sugar

Make the apple sauce as in the previous recipe. adding the grated orange rind and juice. When the apples are reduced to a puree add sugar to taste. and a pinch of salt if you like. At the last moment stir the butter into the hot sauce until it is just dissolved.

Also good with lemon instead of orange. but go easy on the juice.

Spicy Apple Sauce

1 lb cooking apples
1 small onion or 2-3 shallots. finely chopped
1 oz butter
a little brown ale or stout
1 tablespoon cider vinegar
1-2 tablespoons dark brown sugar
nutmeg. cinnamon. pepper. salt

Peel. core and chop the apples and put them in a heavy pan with all the other ingredients. together with 2-3 tablespoons brown ale or stout - or meat stock or water. Cook until soft and beat to a puree. Adjust spices and seasoning to taste.

If this. or any other. apple sauce seems a bit thin. add a few soft breadcrumbs and stir well. If the sauce is too thick. thin with pan juices. if you are serving it with roast meat or game.

Apple and Quince Sauce

1 quince
4 small apples
½ pint cider
3 oz sugar
1 oz butter

Peel, core and coarsely grate the fruit.

Put the grated quince in a small saucepan, pour in the cider and bring to the boil. Simmer for 10 minutes until tender.

Add the apple and simmer for 10 minutes longer. Stir well with a wooden spoon to make a thickish pulp.

Add the sugar and cook gently till melted. Stir well and add the butter.

This sauce goes well with roast pork or goose.

Apple and Horseradish Sauce

1 lb apples
2 oz ground almonds
1 dessertspoon sugar
3 tablespoons freshly grated horseradish
salt and lemon juice or vinegar

Core the apples and bake in the oven.

Skin them and pass them through a sieve.

Stir in the sugar and a little salt. Add enough lemon juice or vinegar to make it smooth.

Add the almonds and lastly the horseradish.

Taste for seasoning. The sauce should be sweet-sour.

Serve cold.

Apple and Onion Stuffing

3 large cooking apples
4 large onions
8 oz cooked potatoes
1/2 teaspoon dried sage
1/2 teaspoon grated lemon rind
pinch of thyme
salt
pepper

Peel and core the apples and chop very finely.

Chop the onion and cook for 5 minutes to soften a little.

Mash the potatoes.

Mix all the ingredients together and season well.

Use to stuff goose, duck or pork.

Nutty Apple Stuffing

3 sticks celery
1 green apple
3 oz chopped nuts
1 large carrot
2 oz butter
2 teaspoons mixed herbs

Mince the celery, apple and carrot.

Melt the butter in saucepan. Remove from heat and add the other ingredients, mixing well.

Season well and use to stuff breast of lamb, or duck, goose, the neck end of a turkey.

Apples Baked with Cream Cheese

Small eating apples, preferably Cox or Reinette,
1 per person
Cream cheese (1 small carton or 1 pack
Philadelphia mashed up with a drop of cream or
milk will stuff 8-10 apples)
Red currant jelly

Core and peel the apples, keeping them whole.
Stuff with the cream cheese, seasoned lightly with
salt, pepper and a scrap of grated orange or lemon
peel if you like it. Dip into melted redcurrant jelly,
and bake in a medium oven until soft. Allow to cool,
and brush with more redcurrant jelly.

Delicious with ham, gammon, roast pork and game.

Salads and Dressings

"The contribution made to European horticulture by skills practiced by monks in the growth and propogation of fruit trees cannot be overestimated."

Walter Horn – The Plan of St Gall

Waldorf Salad

6 tart red apples
2 tablespoons lemon juice
3 sticks sliced celery
3 oz coarsely chopped walnuts
3 tablespoons salad dressing
1 medium sized lettuce

Wash the apples. Quarter. core and dice coarsely without peeling. Toss in lemon juice.

Add celery. nuts and salad dressing or mayonnaise and moisten well.

Serve at once on crisp lettuce.

Apple and Nut Salad

3 crisp eating apples
3 tablespoons lemon juice
2 oz shelled walnuts
¼ pint soured cream
2 oz red cabbage
2 sticks celery
8 large radishes
2 oz seedless raisins
seasoning
4 lettuce leaves

Wash apples and cut into chunks. Toss in lemon juice.

Chop walnuts. reserving a few for garnishing.

Pour cream into a bowl and stir in the apples and nuts.

Shred cabbage finely. slice the celery and radishes.

Stir all into the cream mixture and season well.

Serve on lettuce leaves and garnish with walnuts.

Apple and Raisin Slaw

1 lb white cabbage
1 small onion
4 oz carrots
¼ pint mayonnaise
1 dessert apple
lemon juice
2 tablespoons seedless raisins
seasoning

Discard outer cabbage leaves. Wash and thoroughly dry the cabbage and shred finely.

Finely chop the onion and grate or shred the carrots.

Core and chop the apple and toss in lemon juice. Add to the slaw with the raisins. Mix well.

Apple and Cauliflower Salad

1½-2 thinly sliced unpeeled dessert apples
6 oz thinly sliced raw cauliflower
salt and pepper
mayonnaise (about ⅓ pint)
5-6 lettuce cups

Cut apple slices in thirds, crosswise. Toss with cauliflower and enough mayonnaise to coat each piece.

Season to taste with salt and pepper. (Add a little lemon juice if you like a more tart salad).

Chill thoroughly and serve in lettuce cups. Makes 5 to 6 servings.

Apple, Celery and Turkey Salad

Equal weights of:
Dessert apples - Cox or Reinette
Celery
Cold cooked turkey
3 oz Gruyere for each 1/2 lb meat
Vinaigrette dressing or mayonnaise thinned with a little single cream

Core but do not peel the apples and cut them into dice. Slice the celery, and dice the meat. Cut the cheese into short matchsticks. Mix all the ingredients together and pour over a vinaigrette dressing made with white wine or cider vinegar, a light olive oil or sunflower oil, salt, black pepper and a little mustard.

If watercress is available, serve the salad in a bowl lined with it. If not, sprinkle chopped parsley generously over the top.

A light and refreshing meal for one of the days after Christmas.

Bacon and Apple Salad

8 oz crumbled fried bacon
1/4 pint diced apple
1/4 pint sliced celery or radish
4 tablespoons mayonnaise
4 lettuce cups of watercress

Combine bacon, apple, celery and mayonnaise.

If necessary, sprinkle with lemon or orange juice.

Fill lettuce cups or serve on a bed of watercress.

Cheese and Apple Salad

½ pint chopped red-skinned apple
2 oz Cheddar cheese, cut in ½" cubes
4 tablespoons mayonnaise
1 teaspoon caster sugar
5-6 lettuce cups
½ pint sliced celery
¼ pint diced pineapple
3 tablespoons lemon juice
¼ teaspoon salt

Combine the apple, celery, cheese and pineapple. Stir the mayonnaise, lemon juice, sugar, and salt together until smooth.

Pour over apple mixture and stir until well coated. Chill.

To serve, spoon into crisp lettuce cups.

Makes 5 to 6 servings.

Australian Summer Salad

4 sticks celery
⅛ cucumber
2 dessert apples
1 small lettuce
juice of one orange

Dice celery and cucumber.

Core apples, dice and add to celery and cucumber.

Toss well in orange juice. Chill for one hour.

Wash the lettuce and dry thoroughly. Crisp in the fridge.

Serve the salad on a bed of lettuce leaves.

Yoghurt and Apple Dressing

5 oz plain yoghurt
2 tablespoons apple juice
good pinch ground ginger
good pinch ground cardomum or cinnamon

Add the apple juice gradually to the yoghurt.

Stir in the spices and a little salt to taste.

Apple Pies

"But I, when I undress me
Each night, upon my knees
Will ask the Lord to bless me
With apple pie and cheese."
                              Eugene Field.

19 *Deep dish apple pie*

20 *Spice apple pie*

20 *Holly Hill apple pie*

21 *Apple mince pie*

21 *Ripon apple pie*

22 *Garrion apple pie*

22 *Dutch apple tart*

23 *French apple tart*

23 *Tarte des demoiselles Tatin*

24 *Apple streusel pie*

Deep Dish Apple Pie

1 1/2 lb cooking apples
3-4 oz caster sugar
water
8 oz shortcrust pastry

For this pie you need a deep dish of about 2 pt capacity, with a central support to hold up the crust.

Peel, core and chop the apples, not too finely. Pile them into the dish, sprinkling the sugar over them as you go. Add a little water, to come about 1/3 up the sides of the dish.

Roll out the pastry to a shape about 1″ larger than the top of the dish. Cut off a strip about 3/4″ wide all round, brush with water and arrange round the rim of the dish, dampened side down. Brush upper side with water and put on the lid, cutting a hole for the steam to escape through the centre. Press edges together firmly with the back of a fork. Brush the lid with milk or lightly beaten egg white, sprinkle on a thick layer of caster sugar, and bake for 20 minutes at mark 6/200°C, and a further 20 minutes at Mark 5/190°C.

Various flavourings may be added: a pinch of ground cloves; a quince, grated; 3-4 oz seedless raisins and some grated lemon rind; 2 tablespoons apricot jam. Don't overdo the additions, and enjoy a plain apple pie occasionally. For a blackberry and apple pie use 1 lb apples, about 3/4 lb blackberries, and omit the water.

Spice Apple Pie

1½ lb cooking apples
2 oz sultanas
2 oz brown sugar
grated rind and juice of 1 small orange
generous pinch ground cinnamon
8 oz puff pastry

Another deep dish pie.

Peel, core and chop the apples. Mix with sultanas, sugar, cinnamon and orange rind and put into the pie dish. Pour over the orange juice and cover with the pastry as in previous recipe. Brush top with milk or egg white and sprinkle with caster sugar. Bake 20 minutes at Mark 7/220°C, and a further 20-25 minutes at Mark 4/180°C.

Holly Hill Apple Pie

1 lb cooking apples
1-2 oz sultanas
grated orange rind
3-4 oz sugar
1 oz butter or margarine
1 breakfast cup cake or breadcrumbs
1 teaspoon mixed spice
12 oz shortcrust pastry

Line a shallow piedish with half the pastry.

Mix crumbs, spice, grated orange rind, sultanas and half the sugar, and add melted fat. Spread the mixture over the pastry, and cover with cored, but not peeled, chopped apples, sprinkling them with the rest of the sugar. Cover with the rest of the pastry, and bake at Mark 7/220°C for about ½ hour.

Some interesting variants: mix about 3 oz mincemeat with the crumbs (omit sultanas, orange rind, sugar and fat); omit sultanas and orange rind, halve the weight of apples and add about the same weight of blackberries, with a little extra sugar if they are very sharp; or add blackcurrants.

Apple Mince Pie

1 lb cooking apples
4 oz mixed dried fruit - sultanas, currants, chopped
dates, chopped peel - whatever you have
2 tablespoons golden syrup
generous pinch of mixed spice
12 oz shortcrust pastry

Peel, core and chop the apples, and mix with the dried fruit, spice, and warmed syrup.

Line a pie plate with half the pastry and put the apple mixture into it. Cover with a pastry lid and bake at Mark 6/200°C for 30 minutes.

Note if the dried fruit is very dry either soak for ½ hour in cold tea or water, drain and mix, or add a couple of tablespoons of water to the apple mixture.

Ripon Apple Pie

1¼ lb cooking apples
2 oz farmhouse Wensleydale cheese
3-4 oz sugar
12 oz shortcrust pastry

Line a 9″ pie plate or flan dish with pastry. Peel, core and slice the apples thinly, and arrange them in the dish, sprinkling them with sugar as you go. Top with cheese, grated, and cover with a pastry lid in the usual way. Bake for 30 minutes at Mark 6/200°C.

Lancashire or White Cheshire make acceptable substitutes for Wensleydale, but it then becomes Lancaster or Chester apple pie.

Garrion Apple Pie

3 or 4 large cooking apples
2 oz flour
2 oz medium cut oatmeal
3 oz margarine
2 eggs
2 teaspoons sugar
a little almond essence (optional)
apricot or plum jam

Cream margarine and sugar. Add beaten egg and essence if used.

Sift the flour and add the oatmeal. Add this to the mixture.

Spread the soft paste evenly over the bottom of a shallow pie dish and a little up the sides.

Peel and core the apples and slice in segments like an orange. Arrange the slices in overlapping rows over the paste until it is covered.

Spread the jam over the top and bake for 30 minutes in a moderate oven (Mark 4/180°C). Serve immediately.

Dutch Apple Tart

1¼ lb dessert apples
2 oz sultanas
2 oz chopped blanched almonds
2-3 oz caster sugar
nutmeg, cinnamon
2 tablespoons apricot jam or redcurrant jam to glaze
8 oz shortcrust pastry

Line a 9″ pie plate or flan dish with the pastry.

Peel, core and slice the apples and arrange them carefully on the pastry. They look prettiest in concentric circles.

Mix sultanas, almonds, 2 oz sugar and spices and sprinkle over the apples. Bake for 30 minutes at Mark 5/190°C.

While the tart is baking dissolve jam or jelly in a little water. Sieve over cooked fruit, sprinkle generously with caster sugar and put back into the oven for 2-3 minutes.

Serve cold but not chilled, with cream.

A French Apple Tart

1¼ lb eating apples - can be mixed, including if possible a Cox or a Reinette
1½ oz unsalted butter
1 tablespoon caster sugar
2 tablespoons apricot jam
8 oz shortcrust pastry

Line a 9″ shallow piedish (a china or pottery flute-edged flan dish is ideal) with the pastry.

Peel, core and slice the apples and cook very gently in the butter until they are soft and transparent, but not mushy. Stir in sugar to taste - do not make them too sweet.

Remove apples from the pan with a slotted spoon and arrange them carefully in the pastry case. Bake for 25-30 minutes at Mark 6/200°C, until the pastry is brown and the apples browned on top.

While the tart is cooking warm the apricot jam in the apple juices, diluting with a little water if necessary to make quite a thin sauce. Sieve this sauce over the tart, sprinkle liberally with caster sugar and put the tart back into the oven for a couple of minutes, until the sugar is just bubbling.

Best eaten warm or just cold, but not refrigerated, with cream.

Tarte des Demoiselles Tatin

1¼-1½ lb dessert apples, preferably Reinettes or Cox
4 oz caster sugar
4 oz butter
lemon juice
8 oz shortcrust pastry, made with an egg and a dessertspoon of sugar

For this, a straight sided flan dish is essential. It must be about 1″ deep.

Cover the bottom of the dish with a thick layer of softened butter and sprinkle over it half the sugar.

Peel, core and slice the apples and arrange them prettily on the butter. Sprinkle with a little lemon juice and pour over the rest of the butter, melted and blended with the rest of the sugar.

Cover with the pastry, rolled out and patted into shape. The pastry lid must not lap over the sides of the dish. Bake for 30 minutes at Mark 6/200°C.

Allow to cool for about 10 minutes, and then dish up the tart by putting a large flat serving plate over the dish and turning the whole thing upside down.

Serve warm or cold, with or without cream.

Apple Streusel Pie

8 oz shortcrust pastry
6 dessert apples, preferably Cox or Reinette
grated rind and juice of 1 lemon
2 oz sugar
cinnamon and nutmeg or allspice

Streusel topping
3 oz soft brown sugar
3 oz plain flour, sifted
3 oz butter

Line an 8-9″ flan dish with the pastry and arrange on it the apples, peeled, cored, sliced and tossed in lemon juice. Mix sugar and spices, and sprinkle over the apples.

To make the topping, combine flour, sugar and the lemon rind. Soften the butter and cut it into this mixture until it is like coarse breadcrumbs. Sprinkle over the apples.

Bake at Mark 6/200°C for 15 minutes, reduce heat to mark 4/180°C and bake for a further 20-30 minutes.

Serve cold, with whipped cream.

Hot Steamed and Baked Puddings

"Sir, we could not have had a better dinner had there been a Synod of Cooks."

Samuel Johnson.

25	Apple pudding	**29**	Apple roll
25	Cousin Polly's Pudding	**29**	Eve's pudding
26	Apple roly poly	**30**	Apple oat crumble
26	Toffee apple pudding	**30**	Apple and date crumble
27	Apple raisin pudding	**31**	Apple Charlotte
27	Apple and raspberry nest	**32**	Apple pan dowdy
28	Saint Stephen's pudding	**32**	Apple and almond pudding
28	Brown Betty	**33**	Apple and grape clafoutis

Apple Pudding

Pastry
6 oz self-raising flour
3 oz shredded suet
water to mix (¼ pint or less)

1½ lb cooking apples
3-4 oz caster sugar
a few cloves if liked

Make the suet pastry and line a greased 1½ pint pudding basin with it, keeping enough aside for the lid. Fill with peeled, cored, chopped apples, mixed with sugar and cloves. Damp the edges of the pastry lining and fit on the lid, sealing firmly. Cover with greaseproof paper and a lid of foil or a pudding cloth, and tie down well.

Steam for 2 hours, or in a slow cooker on 'high' setting for 3½-4 hours.

NB All steamed puddings, with or without suet, cook beautifully in a slow cooker. They don't dry out and they don't fill the kitchen with steam. Follow the timing given in a slow cooker recipe book, remembering that is is almost impossible to overcook anything.

Cousin Polly's Pudding

4 oz soft white breadcrumbs
2 oz shredded suet
2 oz sugar (white or brown)
2 oz currants
1 large or 2 small cooking apples, peeled, cored and finely chopped
1 oz candied peel (or grated rind of 1 lemon)
2 eggs, well beaten
2-3 tablespoons milk

Mix all ingredients together, pile into a greased 1½ pint pudding basin, tie down in the usual way and steam for 2 hours, or cook in a slow cooker.

Apple Roly Poly

Pastry
6 oz self-raising flour
3 oz shredded suet
1 egg
water to mix

1 lb cooking apples
2-3 oz caster sugar

Make the suet pastry in the usual way, adding a beaten egg and just enough cold water to give a firm dough. Roll out on a floured board as if for a Swiss roll. Spread with peeled, cored, finely chopped apples mixed with sugar. A few currants, grated lemon peel or spices to taste may be added. Roll up and seal, pinching the ends together firmly, and tie in a well floured pudding cloth. Put the pudding into a large pan of fast-boiling water and boil for about 1½ hours. (It is essential to keep the water boiling all the time the pudding is cooking, or it will go soggy. If you have to add more water, boil it up in a kettle first).

Toffee Apple Pudding

1½ lb cooking apples
6 tablespoons sugar

Pastry
8 oz self-raising flour
4 oz suet
¼ pint water
pinch of salt

2 oz butter
2 oz brown sugar

Cream together the butter and brown sugar and spread thickly round the inside of a 2 pint pudding basin. Make a suet pastry and line the basin with it, keeping enough for a lid. Fill with the apples, peeled, cored and chopped, mixed with the rest of the sugar. Damp the edges of the pastry lining and fit on the lid. Tie down with a cloth in the usual way and steam for 1½ hours. Alternatively, the pudding may be baked at Mark 4/180°C for about 1¼ hours, standing the basin in a dish of water. Or slow-cook on 'high' setting for 3½-4 hours.

Apple Raisin Pudding

8 oz cooking apples
2 tablespoons water
12 oz self-raising flour
1 level teaspoon powdered cinnamon
½ level teaspoon mixed spice
about 4 tablespoons milk
3 oz butter
1 oz chopped walnuts
3 oz stoned raisins
4 oz soft brown sugar
2 eggs

Peel, core and slice the apples and stew in the water. Cook and pass through a sieve.

Sift together the flour, cinnamon, and mixed spice.

Rub in the butter, then stir in the walnuts, raisins, and brown sugar. Mix well with the eggs and the apple puree. Mix to a soft dropping consistency with the milk. Put into a greased basin, cover and steam.

Apple and Raspberry Nest

Pastry
4 oz table margarine
1 oz sugar
3 tablespoons milk
7 oz self-raising flour & 1 level tspn baking powder
1 egg, beaten

Filling
3-4 tablespoons raspberry jam
1 lb cooking apples, peeled and thinly sliced
1 oz demerara sugar

Rub margarine into sieved ingredients and stir in sugar. Mix in egg and milk to form a soft dough. Turn onto lightly floured board. Knead lightly.

Roll out two-thirds of the dough and line a greased 2 pint pudding basin. Wet edges.

Spread jam in the bottom. Add prepared apples and sugar. Roll out remaining pastry and cover the top, pressing down the edges.

Cover with grease-proof paper or tin foil. Steam for 1¾-2 hours.

Serve hot.

Saint Stephen's Pudding

4 oz fresh breadcrumbs
2 oz soft brown sugar
4 oz seedless raisins
2 medium sized cooking apples
grated rind of one lemon
2 oz sifted self-raising flour
3 oz suet
pinch of salt
1 egg
3 tablespoons milk

Combine all the dry ingredients in a large mixing bowl and add the raisins.

Peel, core and grate the apples and add them with the grated lemon rind to the mixture.

Beat the egg into the milk and stir into the pudding mixture.

Butter a 2 pint pudding basin and pour in the mixture. Cover with greaseproof paper and a pudding cloth tied with string.

Steam for 2 hours and serve with custard or brandy butter.

Brown Betty

1 lb cooking apples
4 oz brown breadcrumbs
2 oz brown sugar
2 oz dried fruit (optional)
3 tablespoons golden syrup
1/2 teaspoon mixed spice
rind and juice of one lemon

Peel, core and slice the apples finely. Butter a pie dish and put a layer of slices in the bottom. Cover with crumbs and sprinkle with sugar and spices.

Repeat these layers until the dish is full.

Add the lemon juice and grate the rind on top.

Warm the syrup and pour over. Bake in a moderate oven, Mark 4/180°C, for 30 minutes.

(Alternatively, this recipe can be steamed in a pudding basin for 1 1/2-2 hours).

Apple Roll

2½ cups peeled, chopped apples
½ tsp cinnamon
2 cups flour
1 tsp salt
1 tbsp + 1 tsp baking powder
2 cups syrup
juice of one lemon (optional)
6 tbsp butter
½ cup water

Preheat oven to Mark 7/220°C. Heat syrup to boiling and keep hot in an 8″ square tin. Make a pastry with flour, butter and other ingredients. Roll out dough in oblong to ⅓″ inch thick (approx. 12″ long, 6-8″ wide).

Sprinkle apples, cinnamon and optional lemon over dough. Roll up and pinch edges to seal. Cut into slices about 1½″ wide. Place slices, cut edge down into boiling syrup. Bake for 25 minutes, spoon syrup over the cakes and serve warm with cream.

Eve's Pudding

1 lb cooking apples
2 tablespoons caster sugar
grated lemon rind
1 tablspoon water
a little icing sugar
3 oz self-raising flour
2 oz soft margarine
2 oz caster sugar
1 egg
1 tablspoon milk

Peel, core and slice the apples and pack them into a well buttered 1½ pint pie dish. Sprinkle with the sugar and a little lemon rind. Spoon the water over the top.

Cream together with 2 oz caster sugar and margarine. Beat in the egg and then sift in the flour and mix together.

Spoon the cake mixture over the apple slices and smooth with a knife.

Bake at Mark 5/190°C for 35-40 minutes.

Dust with icing sugar and serve hot.

Apple Oat Crumble

1 lb cooking apples
2 oz brown sugar
3 oz quick porridge oats
2 oz margarine
1 oz brown sugar
1 tablespoon cornflour

Peel, core and slice the apples and put them in a baking dish, sprinkling with 2 oz sugar. Mix together oats, cornflour and the remaining ounce of sugar, and stir in the melted margarine. Cover the apples with this mixture, patting it down firmly.

Bake at Mark 4/180°C for about 35 minutes, until the top is brown and the apples are soft. Serve with cream or custard.

Other breakfast cereals may be used for the topping - cornflakes, a mixture of cornflakes and grapenuts, or muesli base. Sultanas, marmalade, grated lemon rind, may be used to flavour the apples.

Apple and Date Crumble

4 oz flour
2 oz margarine
1 teaspoon cinnamon
1½ lb apples
2 oz sugar
2 oz dates

Sift the flour into a mixing bowl and rub in the margarine. Stir in the sugar.

Peel, core and slice the apples. Chop the dates. Place the fruit in a pie dish and spoon over 2 tablespoons of water and a little sugar.

Sprinkle the crumble over the top and bake for 20 minutes at Mark 5/190°C.

Serve with custard or cream.

Apple Charlotte

1 1/2 lb cooking apples
3-4 oz brown sugar
slices of white bread (7-8)
4 oz butter

These quantities should be enough to fill a 9" square baking tin (about 2" deep) or a rectangular dish of similar capacity.

Remove crusts from the bread and spread thickly on both sides with softened butter. Cut each slice into fingers and line the dish, keeping enough to cover the top. Press the fingers together and push the lining firmly against the sides of the dish. Fill with the apples, peeled, cored and sliced thinly, sprinkling them with sugar as you go. Keep 1 tablespoon of sugar for the top. When the dish is full, cover with the remainder of the bread and dust with sugar.

Bake at Mark 5/190°C until the bread is crisp and golden brown and the apples are soft, about 40 minutes. If the bread starts to burn before the apples are cooked reduce the heat.

There are many delicious variations on this pudding. Use a fruit loaf for the lining (you will probably not need so much sugar). Add grated lemon or orange round and a little juice from whichever fruit you choose. Or add a few sultanas. It is also very good with the lining spread with marmalade as well as butter - do this **after** you have put it into the dish if you don't want to land up with most of it on your fingers!

Apple Pan Dowdy

3 large cooking apples
2 level tablespoons brown sugar
1 level tablespoon golden syrup
¼ level teaspoon grated nutmeg
¼ level teaspoon ground cinnamon
4 tablespoons milk
4 oz self-raising flour
pinch of salt
1 egg
2 oz margarine
2 oz caster sugar

Peel, core and thinly slice the apples. Put into a 7 inch greased cake tin with the brown sugar, syrup, nutmeg and cinnamon. Cover with foil and bake in a moderately hot oven (Mark 5/190°C) for 20 minutes. Sift the flour and salt into a bowl. Beat the egg and melt the margarine. Add the sugar, egg, milk and margarine to the flour and beat well together.

Spoon this mixture on top of the apples and spread evenly. Return to the oven and bake uncovered for a further 30 to 40 minutes.

Turn upside-down onto a serving dish.

Apple and Almond Pudding

1½ lb cooking apples
2 oz soft brown sugar
4 oz butter
4 oz caster sugar
4 oz ground almonds
2 eggs

Peel, core and slice the apples and cook them with the brown sugar and a tablespoon of water until they are quite soft. Put the cooked apple in a buttered dish at least 2″ deep.

Cream butter and caster sugar until light. Beat in the eggs one at a time, and finally fold in the ground almonds. Cover the apples with this mixture, spreading it evenly, and bake at Mark 4/180°C for about 40 minutes. The top should be golden brown. Best served warm, after it has been out of the oven for about ½ hour, which makes it a very useful pudding for parties.

Apple and Grape Clafoutis

2 dessert apples, peeled, cored and sliced
4 oz grapes (the large Spanish red ones, or muscats)
halved and with the pips removed
2 oz flour
2 oz caster sugar
3 eggs
1 pint hot milk
butter
vanilla sugar

Butter a flan dish or cake pan and arrange the apple slices and grapes over the bottom of it. To make the batter, beat together the eggs and sugar, stir in the flour (and a tablespoon of armagnac or calvados if possible), and then the hot milk, beating well with a wooden spoon. Pour the batter over the fruit and bake for 30 minutes at Mark 6/200°C, adding small cubes of butter to the top half way through the cooking time. Remove from the oven, sprinkle with vanilla sugar and serve warm, with or without cream.

Cold Apple Puddings

"Poetic Justice, with her lifted scale.
Where, in nice balance, truth with gold she weighs.
And solid pudding against empty praise."

Alexander Pope.

34 *Swedish apple charlotte*

35 *Danish chocolate apple cake*

35 *Grasmere apple gingerbread*

36 *Spiced apple cheesecake*

36 *Oat apple pudding*

37 & 38 *Apple strudel*

Swedish Apple Charlotte

4 oz fresh white breadcrumbs
5-6 oz butter
4 oz caster sugar
2 lb cooking apples
2 oz sugar
grated lemon rind
2 oz grated chocolate

Melt the butter in a large frying pan and fry the breadcrumbs gently until they are golden and crisp. This will take about ¼ hour: it is important not to hurry them or they will burn. Stir in the caster sugar and leave to cool.

Peel, core and cut up the apples and stew them in 2-3 tablespoons water until you have a thick soft puree. Add 2 oz sugar and lemon rind and cool.

Arrange alternate layers of apple and breadcrumbs in a 2 pint dish. A glass dish or bowl is nice if you have one. Finish off with a layer of breadcrumbs, cover with whipped cream and sprinkle the grated chocolate over the top. Chill well before serving.

For a hot version of this pudding, sprinkle the chocolate over the final layer of breadcrumbs and bake in a medium oven, Mark 4/175°C, for 20-25 minutes. Serve the chilled whipped cream separately.

NB Use good quality dark chocolate, Chocolat Menier or the Dutch cooking chocolate obtainable from good grocers and in many supermarkets.

Danish Apple & Chocolate Pudding

1½ lb cooking apples
3-4 oz caster sugar
grated rind and juice of 1 lemon
6 oz fresh white breadcrumbs
3 oz unsalted butter
2 tablespoons cocoa
2 oz demerara sugar
¼ pint cream, whipped

Peel, core and slice the apples and cook with caster sugar and lemon juice and rind until you have a thick puree. Leave to cool.

Melt the butter in a large heavy pan and fry the breadcrumbs in it until golden brown. The heat should be kept low or the crumbs will burn. The frying process will take about 15 minutes. Mix demerara sugar with cocoa and stir the mixture into the crumbs. Leave to cool.

Put a layer of apple puree in a fairly deep glass dish, then a layer of chocolate crumbs. Repeat the layers, and cover the top with whipped cream. Chill well before serving.

Grasmere Apple Gingerbread

2½ lb cooking apples
6 oz white sugar
2-3 tablespoons water
grated rind and juice of a lemon

For the topping
8 oz plain flour
1 teaspoon ground ginger
4 oz sugar (pale soft brown is best)
4 oz unsalted butter
pinch of bicarbonate of soda

These quantities fill a large (11-12″ diameter) flan dish, and serve 6-8 people.
Peel, core and slice the apples and cook with sugar and water and the lemon rind and juice to make a soft puree. When cold, spread evenly over a large flan dish or a 2½-3 pint capacity pie dish.
To make the topping, sift together the flour, bicarbonate of soda, ginger and a small pinch of salt. Rub in the softened butter until the mixture is like coarse breadcrumbs, and stir in the sugar. Sprinkle this mixture over the apples and smooth the top with a palette knife.
Bake for about 30 minutes at Mark 4/165°C. The crust should be a pale golden brown.
Serve cold, with cream or home-made vanilla ice cream.

Spiced Apple Cheesecake

Filling

1 lb cream cheese (or half cream, half fresh curd cheese - NOT cottage cheese)
2 large cooking apples
2 oz sultanas
3 oz caster sugar
pinch mixed spice and pinch cinnamon
1½ oz butter

Crust

4 oz digestive biscuits
2½ oz butter

Butter a 9″ flan dish. To make the crust, melt about 2½ oz butter in a small pan and stir in 4 oz finely crumbled digestive biscuits. Spread the warm mixture over the base of the dish and pat down well with your hands. Leave to cool.

For the filling, peel core and slice the apples thinly, and cook them very gently in 1½ oz butter until they are quite soft but not reduced to mush. Add sultanas, and sugar and spices to taste.

Put the cheese in a large bowl and whip lightly. If you are using packet cream cheese you may need to add a little fresh cream or top of the milk to enable you to break it up and whip it. Stir in the soft apples while they are still warm. Check the flavouring, adding a little lemon juice if the mixture is too sweet or bland, and pile the filling onto the biscuit base. Chill well.

For those with a very sweet tooth, a layer of melted plain chocolate poured over the base before adding the filling is extra delicious.

Oat Apple Pudding

Fry a cupful of patent oats in 1½ oz butter. When starting to brown stir in 2 dessert-spoons of sugar. Do not over cook - mix well. Cool.

Cut up, or coarsely grate, a cooking apple - sprinkle with lemon juice.

Shortly before serving mix oats and apple. Serve with thick cream.

Apple Strudel

Pastry
½-¾ lb plain flour
1 small egg
oil for brushing
pinch of salt
¼-½ pint of tepid water
2 oz butter
A small quantity of oil added to the water and egg is
an improvement

Filling
2 lb apples
2 oz currants
2 oz sultanas
3-4 tablespoons browned crumbs
2 oz butter
a little oil
brown sugar to taste
½ teaspoon mixed spice
½ teaspoon cinnamon
icing sugar

Beat the egg and add about ¼ pint of the water.
Pour the flour into a bowl and add salt, Mix quickly
with the liquid to make a soft dough, adding more
water if necessary.

Beat on a floured board until thoroughly elastic.

Put into a clean floured basin and cover and put in a
warm place for about 15 minutes.

Roll out the paste as thinly as possible then lay on a
floured cloth. Brush with oil and leave until it
becomes elastic, (10-15 minutes). Then pull gently
from all sides until it becomes as thin as paper.
Brush well with melted butter. Scatter with crumbs
and then add the filling. Roll up. Slide onto baking
sheet. Brush with butter again and bake for 30
minutes in a moderate to hot oven. Dust well with
icing sugar.

Apple Strudel with Short Pastry

Short Pastry
5 oz flour
3 oz butter
yolk of small egg
pinch of salt
2 oz sugar
2 tablespoons milk or white wine

Work with a light touch. Leave pastry to cool for 1 hour.

1 lb cooking apples
1 oz sultanas
little lemon juice
2½ oz sugar
1 egg white

Roll pastry into an oblong. Cover with apple mixture. Fold over pastry from either end. Brush with egg white. Pinch ends together. Brush top with egg white also. Bake at least 30 minutes at Mark 5/190°C. Dust lightly with sugar. Leave to cool.

Apples in Batter

"Coleridge holds that a man cannot have a pure mind who refuses apple dumplings. I am not certain but he is right."

Charles Lamb.

Apple Fritters - I

Batter
4 oz self-raising flour (or plain flour + 1 teaspoon baking powder)
1 teaspoon sugar
pinch of salt
1 egg
¾ pint milk (about)

large cooking apples
caster sugar
oil for frying

Make the batter by mixing the dry ingredients and then beating in the egg and milk. A teaspoon of oil improves the consistency. Beat really well, in a food processing machine if you have one, until bubbles form on the surface. Then set aside for at least an hour.

Prepare the apples by peeling and coring them and slicing them horizontally, into rings about ½" thick.

Heat enough oil in a large heavy pan to cover the bottom generously. When it is really hot dip the apple rings one at a time into flour and then into the batter. Fry over a hot fire for about 1 minute on each side, then reduce the heat and cook for a further 3-4 minutes on each side, turning once. As the fritters are cooked lift them out carefully with a slotted fish server or spoon and put them on kitchen paper to dry. Then transfer to a warm dish and dredge generously with caster sugar. Serve as soon as possible.

Apple Fritters - II

2 crisp dessert apples
2 eggs, lightly beaten
1 tablespoon flour
milk
grated lemon peel
pinch of salt
caster sugar mixed with a pinch of cinnamon, for dusting the fritters

Mix together eggs, flour, lemon peel and salt with enough milk to make a light batter. Beat well, and add the apples, grated or chopped finely. Allow the batter to stand for at least 2 hours.

The fritters may be fried in deep or shallow fat. Whichever method you use, be sure that the frying medium you use (preferably cooking oil) is absolutely clean and tasteless, and drain the crisp fritters on a paper towel before sprinkling them with sugar and cinnamon. Keep hot in a lightly covered dish and serve immediately.

Spanish Apple Fritters

Batter
4 oz plain flour
2 tablespoons caster sugar
beer to mix (about pint)

large cooking apples
2 tablespoons sugar
cognac (or white wine laced with a little brandy)
cinnamon

Peel and core the apples and slice horizontally. Sprinkle with 2 tablespoons sugar mixed with a pinch of cinnamon, and pour over the brandy or wine/brandy mixture. Leave to soak for several hours, or overnight.

Make batter by mixing the flour and the rest of the sugar and beating in enough beer to give a fairly thick smooth cream.

Melt some butter in a thick pan, dip the drained apple slices in the batter and fry until golden brown on both sides. Drain, and serve hot with chilled whipped cream and dark brown sugar.

Date and Apple Fritters

Batter
4 oz flour
2 oz margarine
milk to mix

2-3 cooking apples
3 oz chopped dates
a little sugar if necessary

Make the batter by rubbing the margarine into the flour until the mixture is the consistency of fine breadcrumbs, and then add just enough milk to make a stiff batter.

Peel, core and chop the apples and mix with the chopped dates. You may need a little more sugar if the dates are unsweetened. Grated orange or lemon rind is also a good addition.

Mix the apple and date mixture with the batter and fry in hot fat a tablespoon at a time. A mixture of oil and butter is recommended. Drain, dust lightly with sugar and serve.

Apple Jacques

Pancake batter
4 oz flour
1 egg
milk and water to mix - rather more than ¼ pint
1 teaspoon oil

3-4 dessert apples - Cox or Reinette type
2 oz caster sugar
lemon juice

Make the batter in the usual way.

Prepare the apples by peeling and coring them and slicing them as if for a tart, not in rings. Sprinkle with sugar and lemon juice.

Heat a small frying pan until it is very hot, grease with oil or butter, and pour in a small amount of the pancake batter. Cover at once with a few slices of apple, followed by some more batter. Cook for about ½ minute or until the underside is brown, flip over and cook for another minute or so.

Serve the pancakes flat, sprinkled with sugar.

Harvest Pancakes

Batter
3 oz plain flour
1 egg
¼ pint milk

Filling
1 lb cooking apples
1 heaped tablespoon brown sugar
2-3 cloves or a pinch of ground cloves

Sauce
1 cup cider
2 tablespoons honey or syrup
1 oz raisins (not essential)

Make batter by beating first the egg, then the milk into the flour until very smooth and slightly bubbly. Leave on one side for at least an hour. Prepare the filling by cooking the peeled, cored, sliced apples very gently in a tablespoon or two of water with sugar and cloves. Try to keep the fruit from turning to a puree, but it must be soft and with no surplus liquid.

For the sauce, warm together the cider and honey or syrup, with raisins if liked. A dash of brandy or Calvados is a good addition.

Cook pancakes in the usual way. Fill each one with a generous spoonful of the apple mixture, roll up, and arrange in a dish. Pour over the sauce and serve very hot.

Apple and Lemon Croquettes

4 large cooking apples
6 tablespoons fine breadcrumbs
grated rind of one lemon
2 oz sugar
1 egg
crisp breadcrumbs
fat for frying

Bake the apples in their skins in the oven. While still hot, skin and mash them and add the soft breadcrumbs, lemon rind and sugar. Leave until cold and them make into finger shapes.

Roll the croquettes in beaten egg and coat with crisp breadcrumbs. Fry until golden brown.

Serve hot with custard.

Normandy Apple Batter

1½ lb crisp dessert apples
butter for frying
4 oz caster sugar - or to taste
small glass Calvados (or brandy)

Batter
3 oz plain flour
3 eggs
½ pint milk
nutmeg or a little grated lemon rind

Peel, core and slice the apples and fry gently in the butter, keeping the slices whole. Transfer them to a flan dish or similar shallow oven-proof dish, and sprinkle with sugar. Swirl the Calvados in the pan and pour the buttery mixture over the apples. Leave to soak for an hour or two.

To make the batter, beat the eggs into the milk with a spoonful of sugar and a pinch of salt. Add nutmeg or lemon rind flavouring, and then gradually beat in the flour with a wooden spoon (or do the whole thing in a food processor).

Pour over the apples and bake for 1 hour at Mark 4/180°C. Best served warm, sprinkled with icing sugar, with pouring cream.

Apple Dumplings

3 cooking apples
4 oz brown sugar
2 oz self-raising flour
2 oz oatmeal
¼ teaspoon salt
1 egg
¼ pint milk (approx)
1 oz butter or margarine

Peel, core and chop apples and mix with sugar.

Mix together the oatmeal, flour and salt and add the beaten egg and milk to make a drop batter. Stir in the melted butter.

Mix the apple with the batter, coating every piece.

Grease some baking cups and fill with the mixture.

Bake at Mark 5/190°C for about 30 minutes.

Serve hot with cream.

Apples and Eggs

"I am convinced digestion is the great secret of life."
Sydney Smith.

Witches Foam

3 large Bramley apples
5 oz caster sugar
2 egg whites
2 tablespoons smooth apricot jam
a little Calvados or dark rum

Bake the apples in their skins until they are soft and foamy. Let them cool. When cold, remove the skins and turn the puree into a bowl. Stir in sugar, apricot jam, and liqueur if liked. Beat the egg whites until very stiff and fold them gently into the apple mixture. Serve piled up in glasses, well chilled.

Apple Amber

1 lb cooking apples
4-5 oz sugar
2 eggs

Peel and core the apples, cut them up and cook with about 3 oz sugar and a little water until they are reduced to a puree. Remove from the heat and fold in the beaten egg yolks. Turn the mixture into a suitable serving dish and bake at Mark 4/180°C for about 30 minutes.

Whisk the egg whites and fold in the rest of the sugar. Pile on top of the apples and put back into a cool oven to brown the meringue. Serve hot.

Also good cold. Give the meringue about an hour in a very cool oven, until it is set but not brown.

For a more substantial pudding, cook the mixture in a pre-baked shortcrust pastry case.

Orient Pudding

1 lb cooking apples
4-5 oz fresh white breadcrumbs
3-4 oz caster sugar
2 eggs
knob of butter

Peel, core and chop the apples and stew them with sugar to taste and a little water. Let the puree cool slightly.

Separate the eggs, and add the lightly beaten yolks, with the breadcrumbs and a knob of butter, to the apples. Turn the mixture into a souffle dish and top with a meringue made with the egg whites and 1 oz sugar.

Bake about 30 minutes at Mark 4/180°C.

Apple Meringue

6 cooking apples
1/2 cupful water
a little raspberry jam
pinch of ground cloves or cinnamon
2 egg whites
1 tablespoonful of caster sugar
1/2 cupful sugar

Peel the apples, remove cores and slice thinly. Place in a pan with water and sugar and cloves. Stew very gently until tender. Take from the pan and place in a small pie-dish. Allow to cool.

Whisk the egg whites briskly with the caster sugar until very stiff. Spread a little raspberry jam over the top of the apples. Pile the whisked egg white in heaps on top. Return to the oven for a minute or two to set and brown very slightly.

Serve cold.

Pommes á la Parisienne

6 good sized crisp dessert apples
4 oz vanilla sugar
1/2 pint water
3 eggs
2 oz caster sugar
2 oz ground almonds
redcurrant jelly

Make a syrup with the vanilla sugar and water, and poach the peeled, cored apples in it, turning them over from time to time and being very careful not to break them.

When cooked but still firm lift them carefully out of the syrup and put on a wire rack until they are dry and cool.

Put them in a buttered fireproof dish and fill the cavities with redcurrant jelly.

Separate the eggs. Beat the yolks with the rest of the sugar until light and fluffy. Whip the egg whites until stiff, and fold them and the ground almonds into the beaten yolks. Pour the mixture over the apples, dust with a little vanilla sugar and bake for a few minutes in a fairly hot oven, Mark 6/200°C. They should only need about 10 minutes, until the top is crisp and golden.

Serve at (warm) room temperature.

Apple Mousse

1 1/2 lb cooking apples
2 oz sugar
4 egg whites
2 tablespoons caster sugar
apricot or raspberry jam
liqueur - apricot brandy, Grand Marnier, Kirsch (with raspberry jam)
4 oz sugar for caramel

Bake the apples until quite soft. When they are cool enough to handle remove all the pulp and stir in about 2 oz sugar. Do not make the apples too sweet.

Melt 4 oz sugar with a spoonful of water over medium heat until it turns to caramel, stirring continuously. Use this caramel to coat the inside of a 2 pint mould. Leave it to harden.

Whip egg whites until stiff, fold in caster sugar and then fold the mixture into the apple sauce. Spoon the apple mixture into the mould and bake, standing in a pan of hot water, for about 1 hour at Mark 4/180°C. Allow to cool for about 15 minutes before turning out.

Heat the jam, thin if necessary with a little water, and sieve to remove pips if you are using raspberry jam. Flavour with liqueur, and serve the sauce hot.

Swiss Apple Gratin

1 lb cooking apples
3 oz sugar
3-4 oz Zwieback (biscottes)
1 tablespoon sultanas

Topping
3 eggs
3 tablespoons caster sugar
3 tablespoons curd cheese (or cream cheese thinned
with a little milk, or single cream beaten up with a
little lemon juice)
grated lemon rind

Peel and core the apples, cut them up and stew with the sugar and a little water until you have a smooth thick puree.

Crumble the Zwieback with a rolling pin or in a food processor until they are reduced to coarse crumbs.

Arrange layers of apple puree and Zwieback in a baking dish, finishing with a Zwieback layer. Beat egg yolks, caster sugar and curd cheese together until smooth. Add lemon rind, and pour the mixture over the apple and Zwieback. Bake for about 20 minutes at Mark 4/180°C, until the custard is just set.

Whip egg whites with a little more sugar until stiff. Spoon over the dish and put it back in a cool oven until the tips of the meringue turn brown.

This pudding should be served neither too hot nor too cold.

Meringues filled with Apple Cheese

For 8 good sized meringues
1 lb cooking apples
2-3 oz demerara sugar
knob of butter
1/2 lb cream cheese

Peel, core and chop the apples and cook with brown sugar and a knob of butter until soft and smooth. Allow to cool to room temperature, and then beat in the cream cheese, which should be broken up first with a fork. If you have to use a packet, thin it slightly with a spoonful of milk.

Chill the apple mixture, and when it is really cold put a generous amount into each shell and serve as soon as possible.

Many variations are possible: add a few sultanas, or a couple of spoonfuls of redcurrant jelly, or raspberry jelly or jam, or apricot jam; a pinch of cinnamon may be added, or a few drops of almond essence and a spoonful of chopped nuts.

Apple Mincemeat Meringue

1 1/2 lb cooking apples
4 oz sugar
grated lemon rind
pinch of cinnamon
knob of butter
1/2 lb mixed dried fruit
2 oz shelled chopped hazelnuts (or almonds)
2 large egg whites
4 oz caster sugar

Peel, core and chop the apples and stew them with sugar, lemon rind, a knob of butter and a little water. When quite soft and tender, beat to a puree. Add dried fruit (soaked for 1/2 hour in a little water, or cider, if it is very dry) and nuts. Put the mixture in a large souffle dish, or divide between 6 small souffle dishes.

Make meringue with egg whites and caster sugar, and cover the apple mixture with it. Put in a very cool oven for about 2 hours, until the meringue is set.

Serve cold, with pouring cream, or a custard made with the egg yolks.

Baked and Buttered Apples, Whips, Jellies, Ices

"The art of cookery is no longer the disguising but the revealing of native savours."

Edward Bunyard.

Baked Apples

1 good sized cooking apple per person
demerara sugar - about 1 oz per apple
spices to taste
water

Core the apples but do not peel them. If they are very large, it helps them to cook more evenly and faster to draw a knife round the middle to break the skin. Fill the cores with sugar, mixed with a little grated lemon or orange peel and spices to taste -ground cloves, cinnamon, ginger. Stand the apples in a baking dish which they fill without touching each other, pour in about ½ inch boiling water and bake in a moderate oven, Mark 4/180°C, until soft but not collapsing. Baste them with the juices occasionally.

Serve hot, warm, or cold, with custard, cream, or ice cream.

This is the basic recipe. Possible tasty variations are endless. Try stuffing the apples with dried fruit -raisins or sultanas, chopped dates, mincemeat, chopped dried apricots mixed with a few chopped walnuts or almonds, marmalade, damson jam, red-currant jelly, raspberry jelly or jam. For savoury apples, to eat with roast pork, stuff them with mixed chopped nuts and mint jelly, or fresh chopped mint with a little sugar, salt and pepper. If you are going to eat the apples hot, a small knob of butter on top of the stuffing is a nice addition. Cold sweet black tea can be used instead of water.

Apple Jelly

1 lb cooking apples
1 lemon jelly
2 oz sugar
¼ pint double cream

Peel, core and slice apples and cook with sugar in 3 tablespoons water - puree in mixer. Leave to cool.

Make jelly with ½ pint water. Cool.

Add to apple and lightly whisk in cream. Pour into mould to set.

Buttered Apples

1½ lb cooking apples
4 oz butter
3-4 tablespoons sugar
6 slices white bread
⅓ pint whipped double cream

Peel apples and slice thickly. Melt 1 oz butter in a saute pan and cook as many apple slices as will comfortably fit. Add 1 tablespoon of sugar and cook gently, turning until soft. Lift out with a slotted spatula and keep warm while you cook a second batch, adding more butter and sugar.

Remove the crusts from the bread and cut into rounds, allowing one per person.

When all the apples are done, add more butter to the pan and fry the bread on both sides.

Place the bread on a flat plate and spoon over the apple. Top each pile with whipped cream and serve immediately.

Apple Water Ice

An ice to serve with a dish of game

1 lb cooking apples
3 oz sugar
lemon juice
1 large egg white

Peel, core and slice the apples and cook in a little water until quite soft. Pass through a fine sieve of a jelly bag - the liquid should be quite clear. You should have about ¾ pint liquid; if necessary add a little more water. Bring to the boil and add about 3 oz sugar. Boil for 5 minutes and leave to cool. Stir in a little lemon juice.

Whip the egg white until stiff, and fold in the apple syrup. Freeze, stirring occasionally.

This ice can be flavoured with mint; put a couple of sprigs of mint into a little muslin bag, bang it with the back of a spoon to crush the leaves, and put it into the clear liquid while it is boiling up with the sugar.

Apple Aspic

1½ lb cooking apples
4-6 oz white sugar
lemon juice and a little grated peel
1 dessertspoon powdered gelatine dissolved in
¼ pint water
glace cherries

Make the apples into a puree in the usual way, sweetening and flavouring to taste. You should have about a pint of puree.

Oil a 1-1¼ pint decorative mould, and arrange glace cherries, or other glace fruits, over the bottom. Add the dissolved gelatine to the apple puree and pour into mould. Leave to set and turn out when quite cold and firm.

This is another basic recipe. The amount of gelatine required may vary with the variety and condition of the apples. The aspic needs to be just firm enough to turn out in one piece without being too stiff or tough. Flavourings can be varied; add a little dark rum or other liqueur, use candied orange peel for the decoration and a little orange juice in the puree. Before serving, the aspic can be further ornamented with crushed macaroons or ginger nuts, or grated chocolate.

Serve with a home-made custard sauce.

Apples Saint-Jean

1 apple per person
sugar
butter
apricot or raspberry jam
crushed macaroons, about 1 tablespoon per apple

Core the apples and stuff them with sugar. Put a knob of butter on top of each apple, a few drops of water on each, cover the baking dish with thickly buttered paper and bake in a hot oven, Mark 6/200°C, until the apples are tender. Depending on the size and variety, this may take from 20-35 minutes. Remove the paper, spread a little jam over each apple (if using raspberry, or raspberry and redcurrant, sieve it first to get rid of the pips), and sprinkle the crushed macaroons over the jam. Put back into the oven for 5 minutes. Sprinkle the apples with a little Calvados or brandy, and serve hot.

Baked Apples with Sherry (Spanish)

6 large cooking apples
2 hard boiled eggs
1 teaspoon anisette
5 tbsp medium sweet sherry
4 oz castor sugar
1 oz melted butter

Rinse apples under cold running water. Remove the cores, taking care not to cut deeply into flesh.

Separate the yolks from whites. Pound the yolks to a paste. Add the anisette and mix well. Add the sherry gradually, mixing well after each addition. Stir in sugar and melted butter.

Stand the apples in a shallow baking dish and spoon some of the mixture into the middle of each apple. Bake in a hot oven (Mark 7/220°C) for 30 to 40 mins. If the skins are too brown before they are cooked, lower heat after 30 minutes to Mark 5/190°C and bake for extra 10-15 minutes.

Serve hot or cold.

Apple Whip

1 large can evaporated milk
1 pint apple puree
pinch ground cloves
pinch of coriander
finely grated rind of one lemon

Chill the milk and whip until thick and doubled in volume.

Blend in the puree, spices and lemon rind.

Pour into a serving dish and decorate with a little angelica or chopped cherry.

Serve chilled.

Apple Ice Cream

¾ lb cooking apples, preferably Bramleys
3 oz pale soft brown sugar, or 3 oz honey
pinch of cinnamon
1 teaspoon lemon juice
½ pint whipping cream (or ¼ pint single, ¼ pint
double, stirred together)

Peel, core and chop the apples and cook in a
tablespoon of water until you have a thick smooth
puree. Stir in sugar or honey, cinnamon and lemon
juice and leave to cool. Add a few drops of green
colouring, if you like, or a spoonful of crab apple
jelly, or even redcurrant jelly.

Whip the cream until it is just beginning to thicken,
then stir in the cold apple puree and beat the
mixture until it is really thick. Put into a plastic
container, cover and freeze, stirring occasionally.

NB Like all fresh cream ices, this one will not retain
its smooth texture for long (a month at most), as the
water tends to separate out and form ice crystals. It is
best made one or two days before it is to be eaten.

This ice cream is delicious made with a blackberry
and apple puree. Use ½ lb apples and ½ lb blackberries, cooked and sweetened to taste (no water).

Omit the cinnamon, but add a little lemon juice to
bring out the flavours. Remove the pips by passing
through the finest disc of a Mouli-legumes, beat in
the lightly whipped cream and freeze.

Apple Gratin

Peel tart apples.

Cut into quarters and cook in a vanilla flavoured
syrup, keeping them a little firm.

Strain and dry.

Arrange in an oven-proof dish on a layer of apple
sauce.

Scatter some crushed macaroons on top.

Sprinkle with a little melted butter and brown the top
in a slow oven.

Bread, Scones and Muffins, Cakes

"There was cakes and apples in all the Chapels…"
R. H. Barham

Apple Cake

6 oz self-raising flour
1 teaspoon baking powder
3 oz caster sugar
1 large egg
6 tablespoons milk
1 oz melted butter

Topping
1 lb cooking apples
3 oz caster sugar
1 oz melted butter
cinnamon and grated lemon rind to taste

Sift flour and additional baking powder and stir in the sugar. Beat together egg, milk and melted butter, make a well in the centre of the flour and pour in the mixture. Fold gently until all the flour is incorporated, and then beat hard until you have a smooth, soft mixture. (This cake batter can be made in a food processor).

Grease a shallow oblong tin about 11″ x 7″ (a swiss roll tin is ideal), and spread the batter over it as evenly as possible.

For the topping, brush the batter with the rest of the melted butter, and then arrange the peeled, cored, sliced apples in neat overlapping rows. Mix remaining sugar and flavourings and sprinkle thickly over the apples. A little warmed, thinned, smooth jam or jelly may be poured over the apples first.

Bake at Mark 6/200°C for about 35 minutes, or until the apples are tender and golden. Serve warm or cold, with home-made custard or cream.

Apple Drop Scones

4 oz self-raising flour
1/2 teaspoon baking powder
pinch of salt
1 dessertspoon caster sugar
1 crisp apple, peeled and grated
1 egg beaten in scant 1/4 pint milk

Sieve flour, additional baking powder, salt and sugar. Beat in apple and the egg/milk mixture. Beat well for at least a minute, and cook at once by dropping spoonfuls onto a well-greased hot griddle or frying pan. Turn once during cooking. Cool the scones in a cloth on a wire tray, and wrap until ready to serve, preferably while still just warm, with butter.

Apple Bread

12 oz plain flour, white, or mixed white and
wholemeal
1 teaspoon baking powder
1/2 teaspoon bicarbonate of soda
1/2 teaspoon salt
2-3 eating apples
2 oz chopped walnuts or chopped mixed nuts
3 oz grated Wensleydale cheese
5 oz soft light brown sugar
2 oz margarine
2 eggs

Core the apples but do not peel them. Chop finely in a food processor, or use a coarse grater. Keep as much juice as you can.

Cream margarine and sugar. Add the eggs one at a time, beating after each addition. Stir in the chopped apples and juice, cheese and nuts.

Mix all the dry ingredients together and fold into the creamed mixture. Be careful not to overmix.

Bake in a well-greased loaf tin at Mark 5/190°C for about an hour. Test with a skewer. Cool on a rack, and do not store in a tin until it is absolutely cold, or the apples may turn mouldy.

To be eaten sliced and buttered, or with some more cheese sandwiched between two slices as a perfect picnic food. A few sultanas may be added as well as, or instead of, the nuts.

Apple Muffins

8 oz plain flour
1 teaspoon baking powder
3 oz lard
1 lb cooking apples
1 egg
2 oz black treacle

Sift together flour and baking powder. Rub in the lard.

Peel, core, and chop or grate the apples. Beat the egg.

Make a well in the flour mixture and stir in apples, egg and treacle. Stir until you have a stiff, sticky dough.

Spread the dough on a well-greased baking tray in a hot oven, Mark 8/230°C, for about 25 minutes or until golden brown. While still hot, cut into rounds, or more economically into squares, and cool these on a rack. Serve while still just warm, split open, buttered and dusted with caster sugar, which may be flavoured with cloves or cinnamon or ginger to taste.

Apple and Raisin Loaf

8 oz self-raising flour
pinch of salt
2 oz margarine
2 oz seedless raisins
grated lemon rind
2-3 oz soft brown sugar
½ lb cooking apples, chopped finely or grated
1 egg
milk

Mix flour and salt and rub in the margarine. Add raisins, lemon rind, sugar and chopped apples. Leave the skins on unless they are very tough or badly marked.

Beat egg with 4 tablespoons milk and add to the dry mix.

Bake in a small loaf tin, well greased, at Mark 5/190°C for about 40 minutes.

NB The dough should be firm but not too stiff. The quantity of milk required depends on the juiciness of the apples, and you may need to add another spoonful or two.

Allow to cool completely before storing in a tin, and do not try to keep it for more than a few days.

Toffee Apple Cake

½ pint apple puree, not too sweet
6 oz self-raising flour
3 oz margarine
3 oz sugar
1 egg
milk
4 oz granulated sugar for the toffee covering

Use a 7-8" round cake tin, greased and lined, or bake in individual bun tins. This recipe will fill about 12, depending on their size.

Cream margarine and sugar until light and fluffy. Beat in the egg. Fold in the flour and mix gently, adding just enough milk to give a soft dropping consistency.

Bake at Mark 5/190°C for about 30 minutes, or at Mark 4/180°C for about 15 minutes if you are using individual tins. Turn out of the tin or tins and leave to cool.

Put the cake on a suitable serving plate, or the little cakes in paper cases. Cover with the apple puree, which should be firm.

Heat the granulated sugar with a scant ¼ pint water in a thick pan until it is dissolved, and then boil to the soft ball stage (drop a little into a cup of cold water to test). Spoon some of the toffee over each cake and leave to set. Eat the same day.

Apple Torte

4 oz butter
4 oz caster sugar
2 eggs
6 oz self-raising flour
1 lb cooking apples
4 oz chopped walnuts
½ teaspoon powdered mace
1 tablespoon brandy or cider

Cream the butter and sugar until light and fluffy. Mix in the beaten eggs and flour alternately.

Peel, core and slice the apples and add to the mixture, together with the walnuts, mace and brancy or cider.

Mix all well together and then turn into a buttered square baking tin.

Bake in a moderate oven, Mark 4/180°C for 45 minutes.

Serve with whipped cream laced with a little brandy.

Apple Gingerbread

1 lb cooking apples
12 oz self-raising flour
2 teaspoons ground ginger
6 oz margarine
5 oz soft brown sugar
3 oz golden syrup
3 oz black treacle
2 eggs

For this cake you need an 8″ square tin, greased and lined with paper.

Wash the apples but do not peel them, and grate them up or chop finely in a food processor. Sprinkle with a few drops of lemon juice to stop them turning brown.

Heat sugar, margarine, golden syrup and teacle until the sugar is dissolved.

Sift flour and ginger into a mixing bowl. Beat the eggs and add to the flour, together with the melted ingredients. Beat until smooth, then stir in the apples. Spoon into the prepared tin and smooth over the top.

Bake at Mark 5/190°C for about 1-1¼ hours, until a skewer comes out clean. Allow to cool in the tin for ten minutes before turning out. Dust a little caster sugar over the top.

Very good as it is, it can be made into more of a party cake by lemon or orange icing.

Apple Upside-Down Cake

1 lb cooking apples
6 oz self-raising flour
3 oz soft light brown sugar
3 oz white sugar
2 oz margarine
1 egg
1 teaspoon mixed spice
milk

Use a 7-8″ cake tin, well greased (with butter if possible) but not lined.

Peel and core the apples and cut them into neat slices. Arrange in the bottom of the tin, and cover with the brown sugar mixed with the spices.

Rub the margarine into the flour and add the white sugar. Mix with a lightly beaten egg and enough milk to make a firm dough. Spread this over the apples. Bake at Mark 6/200°C for 35-40 minutes. Allow to cool in the tin for a few minutes, and then put a serving dish on top of the tin and flip the whole thing over.

Serve warm, with cold cream or ice cream.

Apple and Lemon Cake

5 oz self-raising flour
3 oz margarine
3 oz caster sugar
1 egg + 1 egg yolk
1 large cooking apple
1 small red-skinned dessert apple
2 oz soft brown sugar
2 oz lemon curd
lemon juice

Cream margarine and sugar until light and fluffy, then beat in egg plus additional yolk. Fold in the sifted flour.

Spoon into a 8″ round cake tin, greased and floured, and bake at Mark 5/190°C for about 30 minutes, until pale golden brown. Cool on a wire rack.

Peel, core and chop the cooking apple and stew it gently with the brown sugar and a tablespoon of water until thick and soft. Sieve it, or puree in a food processor, and mix with the lemon curd. Spread this mixture over the cake. Decorate with slices of the red-skinned apple, skin left on, that have been tossed in lemon juice, and serve at once.

This looks pretty and tastes good. If you can't get hold of a well flavoured red-skinned apple (a soggy, tough-skinned Red Delicious or Mackintosh won't do), poach the apple slices in a little redcurrant jelly mixed with water for a minute or two, to colour them, and drain carefully before arranging on top of the cake.

Preserves

"Keep me as the apples of an eye."
Psalm 17 – King James Bible.

Apple Jelly

windfall apples or crab apples
preserving sugar
water

Wash the fruit and cut into rough pieces, without peeling or removing the pips. Put into a large pan, cover with water and simmer until the fruit is soft. Strain through a jelly bag into a large basin. If you haven't got a jelly bag, use a closely woven white cloth such as an old pillowcase draped over a colander. Whichever method you use, do not hurry the straining process, and do not be tempted to squeeze the bag or cloth at the end or the jelly will be cloudy.

Measure the juice and use 1 lb sugar to each pint. Boil until setting point is reached, pot and cover.

Crab apples are best used on their own, but if you like you can flavour ordinary cooking apples with a quince or two, or a few cloves and a small piece of cinnamon tied up in a little muslin bag and boiled with the apples. This spiced jelly is particularly good with pork. Leaves of fresh mint, lightly crushed and tied in a bag, make a delicious flavouring for jelly to be eaten with roast lamb.

Spiced Apple Butter

4 lb cooking apples
1½ lb sugar
1¼ pints water
juice of 1 lemon
cloves and a piece of cinnamon stick tied up in a muslin bag

Peel but do not core the apples and slice them up roughly. Put in a pan with water, lemon juice and spices and cook until the apples are a soft pulp. Remove bag of spices and push the apples through a nylon sieve or use the finest disc of a Mouli-legumes. Return the puree to the pan, add the sugar and reheat slowly, stirring to make sure the sugar is fully dissolved. When it is, bring to the boil and cook until the mixture is really thick, stirring frequently. Pot and cover.

Apple and Tomato Chutney

3 lb tomatoes
3 lb apples
1 lb onions
1 green pepper
8 oz sultanas
2 pints spiced vinegar
8 oz soft brown sugar
1 level teaspoon salt
¼ oz root ginger
8-10 red chillies

Skin the tomatoes, peel and core the apples, peel the onions and wash the pepper. Chop finely and mince together.

Place in a pan with the sultanas, vinegar, sugar and salt. Tie the ginger and chillies loosely in a muslin bag and add to the pan. Bring to the boil, stirring until the sugar has dissolved.

Simmer uncovered until the vegetables are soft and the contents of the pan reduced and thickened.

Remove the muslin bag. Pour the hot chutney into hot clean jars and seal.

Spiced Apple Preserve with Dates

4 lb cooking apples
4 lb sugar
1 lb stoned dates
grated rind and juice of 3 lemons
pieces of ginger and cinnamon tied up in a muslin bag

Peel and chop the apples and put them in a large bowl with the lemon juice. Cover with sugar and leave overnight. Next day transfer to a large pan and stir over low heat until all the sugar is dissolved. Add chopped dates and lemon rind and bag of spices, and bring to the boil. Cook for about 25 minutes, until setting point is reached. Remove spice bag, pot and cover.

Mincemeat

1½ lb cooking apples
¾ lb stoneless raisins
¾ lb currants
¾ lb sultanas
¼ lb mixed peel
2 oz chopped blanched almonds
¾ lb suet
¾ lb soft brown sugar or molasses sugar
grated nutmeg, cinnamon, mace (about ½
teaspoon each)
grated rind and juice of 1 lemon and 1 orange
a good tot of brandy or rum

Peel, core and chop the apples into small pieces. Mix all the ingredients together, stirring well. Add the brandy or rum last. Pack tightly into jars, preferably glass preserving jars with clip-on or screw tops. If you have to use jam jars, seal them as tightly as possible with several layers of greaseproof paper tied on firmly.

These quantities make about 6 lb mincemeat, which should keep for several years and improves with keeping.

Granny's Chutney (uncooked)

1 lb onions
2 lb cooking apples
2 lb seedless raisins
2 lb sugar
3 pints vinegar (preferably cider or white wine)
1½ oz ground ginger
2 oz salt
¼ lb mustard seed, lightly crushed

Bring the vinegar to the boil and add ginger and salt.

Chop apples and onions finely. Put them in a large bowl, and stir in raisins, sugar and mustard seed. Pour over the boiling vinegar mixture and stir well.

This uncooked chutney should be kept for at least a month before eating. It needs stirring frequently, once a day if possible. Either leave it in the mixing bowl, with a foil lid, or put it into jars, leaving enough room to stir.

Apple and Apricot Jam

1 lb dried apricots
12 lb apples (use windfalls)
sugar
water

Cut apricots into pieces and soak in as much water as they will absorb.

Wash and cut up the apples without peeling. Boil in a little water until soft. Put the fruit through a sieve. Add the apricots and weigh.

Bring the fruit to the boil. To each pound of pulp allow ¾ lb sugar (or 1 lb sugar to 1 pint of pulp). Boil quickly to setting point. Stir well and bottle.

(The faster the fruit boils, the deeper the colour and the stronger the flavour of the jam).

Apple Chutney

2 lb cooking apples
¾ lb onions
1 lb sugar
3 teaspoons salt
1¼ pints vinegar
½ teaspoon cayenne pepper
4 oz sultanas
2 oz crystallised ginger, chopped
1 clove garlic

Peel and core the apples and chop.

Skin and mince the onions.

Put all the ingredients into a pan and simmer very slowly. Stir often and do not cover the pan.

Cook for 2½ hours until chutney is thick and has no free vinegar on the surface. Pour into hot clean jars and seal.

Apple Curd

2 lb cooking apples
2 eggs
8 oz unsalted butter
8 oz sugar
juice of 1 lemon

Peel, core and chop the apples and stew them in a little water until you have a puree. Sieve if necessary. Add sugar and melted butter, then beat in the eggs and cook slowly for about 30 minutes, preferably over hot water to ensure that the mixture does not curdle or turn into scrambled eggs. When it is thick and creamy, add lemon juice, pot and cover.

Miscellaneous

"...it is even congenial for monks to have the care of a garden, to till the land, and to take interest in a good crop of apples."

Cassiodorus – Institutes

Cottage Cider

10 lb windfall apples
1 lb sugar
1 gallon water
2-3 oz fresh yeast

Include some cider apples, or well flavoured dessert apples, in the brew if possible. If all you have got are indifferently flavoured cookers and eaters, add up to 1 lb raisins at the beginning.

Wash the fruit, and chop up using a stainless steel knife, or grate using a plastic grater. You can use a food processor with a stainless steel blade. Put the chopped fruit (with raisins if liked) into a large earthenware bowl or a plastic bucket. Dissolve the sugar in the water and add. Cover the container and set aside for 3 days, stirring occasionally.

Now add the yeast (if you have to use dried yeast, 1½ oz should be enough, reactivated in a little warm water with a teaspoon of sugar) and put the covered container in a warm place for a few days, until it stops bubbling.

Pour off the clear liquid and strain through muslin to remove any little bits. Strain the pulp through several layers of muslin, or better still, through a jelly bag. This may take several hours. Mix the liquids and pour into large stoppered jars. Set aside in a cool place until the cider is completely clear. Syphon off leaving any deposit behind. Dissolve ¼ lb sugar per gallon of cider, add and stir well. Bottle in champagne bottles, cork them and tie the corks down.

Store for at least 3 months before drinking, on their sides in a cool cellar.

Autumn Apple Toddy

1 lb apples
2 tablespoons honey
1½ pints water
ground nutmeg

Wash apples and chop roughly. Put in large saucepan with water and cook until soft and pulpy. Press apples through a sieve with a wooden spoon. Return pulp and liquid to the saucepan and stir in the honey and pinch of nutmeg. Reheat and serve immediately, sprinkled with a little extra nutmeg.

Dried Apples

Sound, sweet apples may be dried by coring them (leave the peel on) and stringing them in long lines in a warm, dry, airy room. When they are quite firm and dry the strings can be turned into necklaces and the apples hung up in a warm dry place.

Alternatively, where a suitable drying room is not available, the apples should be peeled, cored and sliced into 1/8″ thick rounds (drop them into a bowl of salted water as you prepare them, to stop them discolouring). When you have prepared a batch for drying, pat them dry and either lay them out on baking trays or string them and fasten the strings to the oven shelves. Dry in a very cool oven, not more than 70°C. They may take 12 hours or more; if in doubt, allow them to cool off, check for moisture and if necessary give them another few hours.

When quite cold they may be stored in boxes, but do be sure to check the boxes once in a while in case there is still the odd damp one that will start to go mouldy.

Chopped dried apples are an excellent addition to muesli. Chopped and then soaked they may be used instead of fresh chopped apples in many of the recipes in this book. To cook them, simmer very gently until they dissolve to a soft puree and sweeten to taste. Good for apple sauces and spicy apple puddings, where the inevitable darkening of their colour doesn't matter.

Apple Muesli with Yoghurt

2 dessert apples
2 tablespoons honey
1/2 pint natural (unsweetened) yoghurt
2 tablespoons lemon juice
4 oz mixed grains (can be bought in most health food stores as muesli base)

Core the apples, leaving the peel on them, and chop finely. Pour lemon juice over them. Add yoghurt and honey, and a little water if the mixture is very thick. Stir in the mixed grains and allow to stand for few minutes. Turn the mixture into a serving dish and sprinkle with mixed nuts, if liked, and a little demerara sugar.

Crab-Apple Wine

4 lb or more crab-apples
8 pints boiling water
wine-makers yeast
juice of 1 lemon (optional)
3 lb sugar

Roughly chop up apples - cores, stalks and all into a pail or large bowl. Vessel must be pottery or plastic, not metal.

Pour on boiling water, stir well.

Leave to stand for four days, stirring well daily, crushing the apples to get out as much juice as possible.

Strain off the juice onto sugar, add yeast and lemon juice if used.

Put into fermenting vessel.

Leave to ferment in a fairly warm atmosphere -kitchen ideal. May be vigorous at first, so watch it.

Rack when ready, at least once.

Bottle when clear. Keep at least six months.

Charoset

The mortar used by the Children of Israel when they built the pyramids for Pharoah in Egypt - a Jewish sweetmeat

3 dessert apples
3 oz blanched almonds
1-2 oz seedless raisins
sugar
cinnamon
a little port or sweet wine - altar wine is ideal
icing sugar for coating

Peel, core and grate the apples. Chop the almonds very finely - until they are like coarse breadcrumbs -and chop the raisins. Mix together well, and flavour with cinnamon and a little sugar, about a tablespoon. Moisten with the wine until you have a thick, granular paste.

This may either be eaten as it is, spread on matzo or zwieback, or alternatively form little balls of the mixture, roll them in icing sugar, and pile them up in a small bowl, to be handed round at the end of the meal.

Toffee Apples

12 medium-sized dessert apples
12 wooden skewers
6 oz golden syrup
12 oz soft brown sugar
1 oz butter
1 teaspoon cider or white wine vinegar
¼ pint water

Wash and dry the apples, remove their stalks and push a wooden skewer into each one.

Put remaining ingredients into a heavy saucepan and heat gently, stirring continuously, until the sugar is dissolved. Then bring to the boil and boil rapidly to 145°C (290°F), or until a drop in cold water sets hard and snaps cleanly.

Dip apples in the toffee one by one, twisting them about to ensure they are completely covered. Immediately dip in iced water, and then stand on a buttered baking tray to set.

NB Dipping and cooling need to be done very fast: it helps to have an assistant. The apples should be wrapped in waxed paper if they are not to be eaten at once, to preserve the crispness of the coating.

Oat Crisp

This recipe does not contain any apples, but it is very useful for preparing apple dishes such as crumbles, baked apples, open apple tarts

8 oz quick cooking oats
4 tablespoons demerara sugar
3 oz butter, preferably unsalted

Melt the butter slowly in a large saucepan. Do not let it fizzle and boil. Stir in the other ingredients. Sprinkle the mixture over the bottom of a large shallow tin, such as a swiss roll tin (ungreased). Cook for about 10 minutes at 165°C, Mark 4, stirring once or twice to break up any lumps.

Leave to cool. When quite cold crush with a fork, or put between two sheets of greaseproof paper and run a rolling pin over it until the mixture is like coarse crumbs. Store in an airtight jar. Keeps well in a cool dry place.

Apple Ointment

1 lb flead
1 lb apples
1 oz cloves
½ pint olive oil
½ pint rosewater
juice of 2 lemons and grated lemon peel

Slice the flead and put it into an earthenware pippin with the lemon peel and cloves. Add the apples, coarsely chopped, peel, cores and all.

Cook in a very slow oven for about 3 hours, or in a slow cooker for 10-12 hours.

Strain the melted fatty liquid through several layers of butter muslin, add oil, lemon juice and rosewater and stir well. Leave it to stand for a few hours and then pour into jars.

Flead, the very fine, pure lard obtained from the inner membrane of the pig's body, may be difficult to obtain even from a country butcher unless he has his own slaughterhouse. The next best thing is lard prepared by a butcher. Melt it very gently and skim off any impurities before adding the chopped apples and lemon peel.

Muesli

For each helping

1 heaped tablespoon mixed grains
½ apple, grated
1 teaspoon honey
raisins and nuts to taste (hazel nuts are the classic addition, but almonds or walnut pieces are also very good)
lemon or orange juice
water

The grains should be mixed with a little water and left for a few minutes until they are slightly soft but not soggy. Some recipes suggest leaving them overnight, but this tends to destroy the crunchy texture that is part of the attraction of muesli.

Mix in the other ingredients, and serve with milk, or better still single cream. A spoonful of Nestle's milk (evaporated, not condensed) can be added, but not everybody likes the taste.

Index

RECIPES

RECIPES

RECIPES

RECIPES

RECIPES

RECIPES

RECIPES

RECIPES

RECIPES